Critical Guides to Spanish Texts

EDITED BY J. E. VAREY AND A. D. DEYERMOND

KU-533-692

Critical Guides to Spanish Texts

9 Leopoldo Alas : La Regenta

LEOPOLDO ALAS

La Regenta

John Rutherford
Fellow in Spanish, The Queen's College, Oxford

Grant & Cutler Ltd *in association with*
Tamesis Books Ltd 1974

© Grant & Cutler Ltd., 1974
ISBN 0 900411 77 5
Printed in England at
The Compton Press Ltd., Salisbury, Wilts,
for

GRANT & CUTLER LTD
11 BUCKINGHAM STREET, LONDON, W.C.2

Contents

To the memory of W. G. Chapman

Preface

All references to the text of *La Regenta* are to the edition by
Alianza Editorial (Madrid). Each reference gives the chapter
number followed by the page. In quotations, a diagonal stroke
indicates a paragraph ending.

The italicized figures in parentheses refer to the numbered
items in the Bibliographical Note. In it I have listed only published works; otherwise prominent places would have been
occupied by the D.Phil. theses of G. G. Brown (*The Novels and
Cuentos of Leopoldo Alas*, Oxford, 1962) and Jonathan Culler
(*Structuralism: a Study in the Development of Linguistic Models
and their Application to Literary Studies*, Oxford, 1972), the
former as the most complete discussion of Alas's literary work so
far produced, the latter for its close examination of the theoretical
aspects of literary study, and above all for its development of the
concept of "literary competence".

I. *Introduction*

La Regenta is set in the provincial capital Vetusta, a city which, as its name suggests, has a long and noble history that contrasts with its present state of stagnation and mediocrity. Vetusta can be identified with the capital of Asturias province, Oviedo, where Alas lived most of his life as a university professor and professional literary critic. In the aristocratic quarter of Vetusta lives Ana Ozores, beautiful and intelligent, and bored and frustrated by her environment and by her husband Víctor Quintanar, an older and duller man who can satisfy none of her physical and mental needs. The novel tells of Ana's search for fulfilment, which draws her towards two other men: Alvaro Mesía, the local philanderer, and Fermín De Pas, an attractive, ambitious young canon who, at the beginning of the story, becomes Ana's confessor. Eventually Ana falls into Mesía's arms. The jealous De Pas arranges for Víctor to discover his wife's adultery; in the duel which follows Mesía kills him. The scandal breaks and Ana is left facing a bleak future almost friendless and alone.

Even though its story is simple and, in broad outline, hardly original, *La Regenta* is a complex novel as well as a long one. This short *Critical Guide* can, therefore, make no pretence to be exhaustive. I shall concentrate on the text itself, leaving aside questions of its external relationships (with the society of its time, with the national literary traditions to which it belongs, with its literary, philosophical and ideological sources, with the life, intentions and other works of its author). I do not wish to imply that none of these subjects is worthy of attention; but simply that it seems to me that literary study does well to start with the literary phenomenon itself, and with a serious attempt to understand its working. My approach will, therefore, be analytical and non-historical; I shall try to indicate how *La Regenta*, as an organized system, communicates its meanings to its readers, who, to read and understand it, do not need to be aware of the particular causes or circumstances of its writing. The question that interests me is not "How did it come to be?", but rather "What is it?"

Literary communication is obviously linguistic communication plus something else; it is this "something else" which distinguishes literature from all other types and uses of language and thus defines it, and which should therefore be a central concern of literary studies. What is at work in literary communication in addition to what goes on in all verbal communication? To take a simple brief example from *La Regenta*, how is it that the experienced reader of literature has no difficulty in making sense of the logical absurdity of the description of De Pas's manner in terms of "humilde arrogancia"? (XXII, 472). How is it, furthermore, that not only does he make sense of it, but also that the sense he derives seems richer and fuller than any which a description of a more reasoned, precise, ordered sort could give? This is a problem of language, yet linguistics does not, as far as I am aware, give much help in its solution; for paradox is part of the specific language of literature, one of the figures of speech which contribute towards that "something else" that we could call "literariness". Thus, just as modern linguistics is concerned with what Chomsky has called "linguistic competence", so the analytical study of literature should investigate "literary competence", which rests on the foundations of linguistic competence, and yet is quite different. What follows is, then, intended not only as a guide to the working of *La Regenta*, but also (in a partial, tentative, and indirect way) as a guide to the working of narrative literature as a whole.

My immediate goal, however, is *La Regenta* itself. I shall analyse it in terms of categories that have frequently been used in novel criticism: *characterization* (the depiction of man), *story* (the depiction of his development in time), and *setting* (the depiction of his situation in space); but within each of these categories I shall seek, as far as possible, specifically literary principles of organization, for to talk about literature, even realistic literature, in the same terms as one talks about life cannot be expected to add much to our understanding of literariness. I shall therefore try, as far as possible, to avoid talking in psychological or sociological terms about characterization, in historical terms about story, in geographical or even ecological terms about setting. My

aim is rather to discuss, first, the ways in which the text's themes
are embodied and arranged in each of these three areas, and
secondly, the ways in which the whole is presented. This latter
aspect of the text – the manner of presentation of the fictional
world as distinct from that world itself – I shall refer to as
narrative mode. These distinctions are not, of course, ones that
can be made with absolute precision, but they provide a useful
general conceptual framework for the study of narrative texts.
The fact that categories overlap does not invalidate them.

In my discussion of *La Regenta* I shall not be much concerned
to evaluate it. My choice of this work as a subject for analysis
implies in itself that I consider it a splendid novel. My discussion
has a better chance of seeming to achieve a modicum of rigour if
I leave my praise, for what it is worth, at that; and so my general
policy is to leave readers to form their own critical judgments.

II. *Characterization*

Little progress can be made towards an understanding of the way
novels work by talking about characterization solely in terms of
how convincing or lifelike it is. The critic's definition of lifelike-
ness depends on his personal view and experience of life. Eoff
(*14*), for example, finds Ana a weak and unconvincing character;
most readers, I feel, would disagree with him; but this type of
argument tends to reveal more about its protagonists than about
its subject. If our goal is as objective and accurate as possible a
knowledge of the way the system of characterization works in
this novel and, ultimately, in novels generally (not, of course, the
only valid goal, but surely one worth pursuing), we shall have to
find other ways of talking about it, based on an observation of the
specific and distinguishing qualities of literature. I shall work on
the principle that the core, as it were, of a literary text is formed
by its themes; for the ultimate purpose of a work of literature is
to communicate an individual vision of life, in other words a
bringing together in a particular pattern of a certain selection of
themes. Literary characterization could, then, be seen as a permutation of themes. Let us try this idea out in practice.

A consensus of published opinion about the vision of life
presented in *La Regenta* could be stated in the following terms:
Man seeks to direct his life towards spiritual fulfilment, but he is
disastrously unsuccessful because he lives in a world of hypocrisy
in which spiritual activities have been debased and converted into
material and worldly activities. The themes involved here could
be conveniently formulated as four pairs of opposite concepts:
control/abandon, fulfilment/frustration, sincerity/hypocrisy, and
spirit/matter. I therefore suggest these as the principal themes of
La Regenta: the focal points around which its vision of life re-
volves, the particular areas of experience towards which it directs
the reader's attention. Many other themes certainly appear, but I
would argue that they play a subordinate role. It is in terms of
these four themes that I shall now discuss the novel's characters.

Control/abandon.

The world of *La Regenta* is a world of coldly calculating individuals, who normally make a careful point of assessing the likely results of an action before performing it. Enthusiasm, impulse, passion are suppressed, as each character tries to keep charge of his destiny, by making his passage through life go in the direction he wants it to; this is true not only of the three major characters (Ana, De Pas, Mesía) but also of many of the minor ones. The characters often assess themselves and criticize their own behaviour : self-awareness becomes an important part of self-control. But at points of crisis these capacities are liable to weaken. Characters deceive themselves; enthusiasm, passion and impulse get the better of them, and they take unpremeditated steps, though control is subsequently re-established.

Mesía, of the main characters, is the one who most successfully maintains his control over events and over himself. His cynically calculated and executed "scientific" seduction of Ana works, in the end, exactly as planned. Only momentarily is his control threatened, as in chapter XX; now that Ana seems to have slipped from his grasp, he behaves in an unusually impulsive way at the dinner for Guimarán, and nearly gives himself away in the brief interview with Ana which closes the chapter.   P 437.

In De Pas the struggle between control and abandon is more intense. At the beginning of the novel he appears as a character used to exercising complete dominance over himself and the society in which he lives. As the novel progresses, and especially in its second half, his relationship with Ana undermines his domination of self and others. In chapter XII, for example, De Pas is shown going about his normal daily business of organizing others' lives to his own advantage and playing in society the role he has chosen for himself, at the same time as he barely resists the pressures brought to bear on his control by his conscience, re-awakened by his contact with Ana and his hope that under her influence he might become a better priest. His domination of himself and others (including Ana herself) is repeatedly made subject to stress after this point; after each crisis the domination is restored (see especially chapters XIV, XVII, XXI and XXVI). His self-awareness falters, too, as (up to XXII, 474) he persists in deluding himself about his feelings for Ana. And the struggle within him continues, the forces evenly matched and neither able to achieve a definitive triumph, to the very end of the novel. De Pas's inner conflict becomes particularly intense at the climactic moment of Petra's revelation of Ana's adultery, when by a huge effort of the will he manages to impose control on himself (XXIX, 625-6); during his subsequent interview with Víctor (XXX, 644-56), brought about by De Pas in a moment of blind impulse, but then exactly directed in its course by his will; and at the final encounter with Ana (XXX, 675), where the tension between control and impulse is greatest, as De Pas fails to hide his feelings, yet just manages to restrain himself from attacking Ana. His path through the novel, seen in terms of the theme of control, is a constant dialectic which is, as a true dialectic, never resolved.

Ana's control is more precarious than that of either of the two men, though she makes insistent efforts to establish it. She has had little difficulty in keeping herself aloof from all around her, and thus reaching her eminent and envied position in the society of Vetusta; her downfall, indeed, is caused by her over-estimation of her ability to control her feelings and actions, which induces her to court the danger she knows Mesía to offer, because it provides a break from the monotony of her life (XIX, 402-3). Yet Ana, a hypersensitive and imaginative woman, is liable to be carried away by a general, undefined enthusiasm, a vague but overwhelming love for all creation in which the religious and the profane are intimately confused (see particularly the theatre scene in chapter XVI, and the Christmas Mass in chapter XXIII). Her relations with De Pas are characterized by an ebb-and-flow movement, between steps taken in moments of elation (such as her barefoot appearance in the Easter procession) which bring her dangerously close to him, and the subsequent regret and recantation when she is able to see things more clearly. Ana's career in the novel, then, takes the form of an even more agitated dialectic than that of De Pas; it is accompanied by a growing fear of madness, the ultimate loss of control.

Ana's self-awareness is acute but it, too, is liable to falter. She behaves characteristically when, in the course of a conversation with De Pas, she notices that she is using inappropriately rhetorical language and checks herself (XVII, 358), just as De Pas, in a subsequent conversation between the two, realizes that he is using a similar sort of rhetoric but deliberately persists with it, since it is having the desired effect on her (XVIII, 378). But there are limits to her self-knowledge, and self-deceit gets the better of it on the subject of her relations with the two men : thus she makes a close analysis of her nightmare (XIX, 398-9; XXI, 443), and appreciates the sexual significance of its imagery – yet she deceives herself about the key detail, failing to see that the larvae dressed as priests represent De Pas. And only when it is too late, for Mesía has by now had ample opportunities to make inroads on her sensibility, does she come to a proper realization of the strength of her sexual impulses (XXII, 475). To the very end of the novel the tension between a self-aware control and a self-deluding abandon continues in Ana (see especially chs. XXV and XXVII); in the scene immediately before the seduction she is now fully aware of the workings of the dangerous dialectic, and decides to cut it short, by avoiding any more extreme reactions (XXVIII, 604). But it is too late.

In other characters the same theme is worked out on a minor scale. Petra, for example, is a key secondary figure; she, like Mesía and Doña Paula, is one of the characters who most coldly and cynically manipulate events and people, and most successfully achieve what they want. Doña Paula's "seduction" is a characteristic little scene (XV, 308), with its deliberate calculation on both sides and its total absence of passion. Of all the characters, Obdulia is the notable exception, a creature of impulse; her partner Visita is, in contrast, a typical schemer. Even poor Quintanar, whose life is controlled by others throughout most of the novel as completely as if he were a puppet, has occasional, painfully accurate insights into himself (XIX, 393; XXIX, 631-9); and after the disaster he stubbornly refuses to go in the way he is pushed. The opposition awareness + control/delusion + abandon is ironically synthesized in brief descriptions of carefully rehearsed gestures which, it is stated or implied, do not quite produce the desired effect. Visita's flirting with the shop-assistant is one example among many : "clava en el mancebo los ojos risueños, arrugaditos, que Visitación cree que echan chispas. El

catalán finge que se deja seducir por aquellos ojos . . ." (IX, 175 :
see also I, 30; VIII, 150; XI, 213; XXIV, 511). A similar function
is fulfilled by descriptions of the characters' deliberate but imperfect emulation of models, often taken from literature : Víctor
imitates the actor Perales, who in turn imitates Calvo (XVI, 343-
4); the lower classes ape the manners of the local aristocracy (IX,
171; XI, 213; XXI, 442), and the latter copy those of Madrid
(XVI, 337-47); Ronzal imitates Mesía, in turn a counterfeit Don
Juan; Celedonio attempts, when he considers it opportune, to
reproduce the pious looks of priests (I, 11); Ana imitates Santa
Teresa (XXI, 443, 455), and her appearance in the Easter procession is a copy of what she once saw in a similar procession in
Saragossa (XXVI, 551-3).

Fulfilment/frustration

Most of the characters, in one way or another, feel dissatisfied
with their environment, Vetusta, and aspire to something more
stimulating or more rewarding. Durand (6) has shown how they
turn to literature in the course of this quest, seeking in its pages
not only models upon which to base their own behaviour but also
an escape into a world of richer experience. Here, however, they
find only temporary relief and vicarious excitement; the quest for
fulfilment is a vain one for all except two minor characters,
Bishop Camoirán and, on his deathbed, Pompeyo Guimarán.
These two alone enjoy a sense of inner peace and happiness, as a
result of having unreservedly embraced a simple, heartfelt, spontaneous Christian faith which leads them not to worry about the
things of the world. In the face of the self-seeking of others they
are passive, and the other members of Vetustan society scorn
them and use them for their own ends. But in Camoirán and
Guimarán there is the only hint in this novel of a positive solution
to the questions it poses.

Baquero Goyanes (*19*) has argued that Frígilis is another
character who has found fulfilment; not, of course, in the Roman
Catholic faith but in a rejection of urban civilization and its
values and a dedication to the natural life of the countryside. It is
certainly true that Frígilis is one of the characters that the reader
is invited to look on most benignly; but he is presented in a more

ambivalent light than Baquero Goyanes has noticed : he is no simple nature-lover, standing straightforwardly for the health and vitality of the outdoor life. A technique is used for his depiction which, as we shall see, is employed extensively in *La Regenta* : that of giving, rather than a definitive description by the omniscient narrator, a series of partial visions from the standpoints of other characters, out of the combination of which Frígilis himself emerges. This technique itself makes for complexity and ambivalence, for these other characters may be mistaken : Ana, for example, sees him as an inopportune meddler with nature rather than a lover of nature, and considers that he has been no more able to avoid the brutalizing influence of Vetusta than anyone else (XVIII, 380); yet at this moment she is feeling bitter about him for his part in marrying her to an inadequate husband. But although her vision of Frígilis may be a distorted one, there is support for it in other places in the text, where he appears puerile in his petty rivalry with Quintanar (XVII, 370; XIX, 392) and his pseudo-scientific experiments (X, 185, 189; XIX, 390; XXI, 456; XXVII, 569; note, however, that in each of these places the information comes not from the narrator but from another character). Víctor is under great stress and therefore highly unreliable when he comes to accept Frígilis's naturalistic philosophy, which reduces man to the level of all other living matter (XXIX, 638; see also XVIII, 374 and XXI, 453); the narrator characteristically refrains from making any comment in his own voice about the accuracy of Víctor's judgment. Even when, especially in chapter XXX, Frígilis appears in a favourable light, there are limits to what he can offer : "llegó un día en que ya no le bastó [a Ana] vegetar al lado de Frígilis, viéndole sembrar y plantar en la huerta y oyendo sus apologías del Eucalyptus" (XXX, 673 : compare with the ambiguous passage on XIX, 405, where Ana sees Frígilis as an "árbol inteligente" and "encina venerable"; and with Víctor's talk on XXVIII, 605 about "tu vida de árbol secular"). Frígilis is an enigmatic and elusive character, and it is dangerous to attempt any clear-cut definition of him; he cannot be regarded as a simple illustration of the idea of fulfilment through naturalism.

Like Camoirán and Guimarán, both Ana and De Pas look towards religion for fulfilment. Ana's deprived childhood and her unfortunate marriage, together with her exceptional sensitivity and intelligence, make her feel frustration more acutely than any other character. She feels sure that if only she had known the love of a mother, a husband, or a child, her problems would never have arisen. She sometimes – as during the performance of *Don Juan Tenorio* in chapter XVI – sees her relationship with Mesía as a search for fulfilment through profane love; but in a more sober state of mind she realizes that it is little more than a reckless attempt to break the monotony of everyday life in Vetusta by courting danger. Like other characters, Ana looks for fulfilment to literature, particularly to the works of Santa Teresa, whom she tries, in vain, to emulate (see below, p. 28). But it is in her relationship with her new confessor that she places her greatest hopes, which are shattered as the sordid truth about it is revealed, and she sees that this path no more leads to redemption than does any other that is open to her.

In her attempts to identify the goal she is confusedly striving towards, Ana makes frequent use of a word which thus comes to have a special, private meaning in this text: the word is *poesía*, also used occasionally by the narrator and the other characters. An examination of the contexts in which it appears in the novel shows it to synthesize all the vague hopes for some intensely and deeply felt love, whether profane or religious, that will give meaning to life and fulfilment to the individual. It is used to refer to Ana's relationships with De Pas – "aquel hombre que le había halagado el oído y el alma con palabras de esperanza y consuelo, con promesas de luz y de poesía" (XIII, 265) – and with Mesía – "Los pies también seguían su diálogo, diálogo poético sin duda . . . porque la intensidad de la sensación engrandecía la humildad prosaica del contacto" (XXIV, 519). *Poesía* and *poético* appear with especial frequency in the theatre scene in chapter XVI, where they refer to Ana's enthusiastic reactions to the erotic intensity of *Don Juan Tenorio*. In an expression like "el chorro abundante de poesía que había bebido en el poema gallardo, fresco, exuberante de hermosura y color del maestro Zorrilla" (XVI, 347), *poesía* has three concurrent meanings: the normal literal meaning, the normal metaphorical meaning ("great beauty"), and the particular metaphorical meaning it has in this text. There are similar descriptions of Ana's fervent response to the organ music at the Christmas Mass in chapter XXIII. In contrast with *poesía*, *prosa* stands for all that is associated with the humdrum, even sordid reality of everyday life in Vetusta at the present time. *Poesía* is thus illusion, *prosa* reality; one of Ana's mistakes is to overestimate De Pas and Mesía and, in moments of intense feeling, to associate them with *poesía*. Another word that occurs frequently in *La Regenta* and acquires a special meaning in it is *romántico*; it refers to those few remnants of a past age of *poesía* that are left in these present times of *prosa*, and to those few individuals who still cherish this disappearing *poesía*. Romantic attitudes, like those of Ana, are, consequently, noble but doomed to failure, for the world of *poesía*, exemplified in the principal Spanish Romantic drama, Zorrilla's *Don Juan Tenorio*, is an illusory world of the past. The word *romántico* has, indeed, itself been debased and is commonly used in a derogatory sense: "Nada más ridículo en Vetusta que el romanticismo. Y se llamaba romántico todo lo que no fuese vulgar, pedestre, prosaico, callejero" (XVI, 327: the passage continues with some interesting and significant detail).

The "amor universal" (XVII, 362-3) that Ana tries to locate is, then, nowhere to be found in Vetusta; her negative vision of God as "una divinidad oculta, burlona como un diablo" (XVI, 329; XXX, 667) seems to be vindicated, to the detriment of the idea she had entertained in happy moments of "una voluntad superior, que regía la marcha de los sucesos, preparándolos, como experto autor de comedias, según convenía al destino de los seres" (XVI, 338-9), "presidiendo amorosamente el coro de los mundos" (XXI, 455; XXIII, 494). This is an aspect of the work studied by Eoff (*14*). Ana's quest for *poesía* leads only to *prosa* at its vilest, the degradation of the final scene in the cathedral.

De Pas, in turn, hopes that the salutary influence of Ana will make it possible to put his unworthy past behind him, and become a good priest; but he comes to realize, first, that he is too firmly established in his routine of exploitation and domination of others to be able to change (especially in chs. XI and XII) and, secondly, that his feelings for Ana are not totally spiritual. His plan for mutual salvation – "yo la salvo a ella, y ella, sin saberlo por ahora, me salva a mí" (XVI, 331) – fails disastrously. It seems to be implied that fulfilment, which is made synonymous with the Roman Catholic faith, cannot be attained through the mediation of another, for this human intervention inevitably brings with it profane feelings which defile religious ones.

Sincerity/hypocrisy

In the world of *La Regenta* the spoken word rarely communicates thoughts in any direct way. It often contradicts them: De Pas, in order to excite Víctor to avenge himself on Ana and her lover, pleads with him, with hypocritical insistence, not to do so (XXX, 652-4). The language of genuine communication is more often unspoken implication and gesture, especially movements and expressions of the eyes; the scene between Ana, Mesía and Víctor at the beginning of chapter XXIX (610-11) is characteristic, with its rapid succession of messages conveyed in a devious and concealed way by looks and gestures. Attention is unfailingly directed towards characters' eyes in descriptions: "En los ojos del Magistral, verdes, lo más notable era la suavidad de liquen; pero en ocasiones, de en medio de aquella crasitud pegajosa salía un resplandor punzante, que era una sorpresa desagradable, como una aguja en una almohada de plumas" (I, 12). The eyes of all characters, even minor ones, receive similar emphasis; for the eyes are silent and therefore truthful witnesses to a character's nature and thoughts, which he normally hides in his effort to control his public behaviour. The lustful village priest Contracayes is "moreno, de cejas muy pobladas, ceño adusto, ojos de color de avellana que echaban fuego, boca grande . . ." (XII, 245).

The characters are aware that what is said to them by others is likely to be the least important thing; in conversations there is often, consequently, an extra-linguistic level at which real communication takes place. Examples are numerous: the "pacto de sordomudos" between Ana and Mesía (IX, 179-80); the conversation between De Pas and Somoza (XII, 224); the eloquent exchanges of looks between Mesía and De Pas (XIII, 277; XXV, 531-2; XXVI, 559); the expressive look with which De Pas accompanies his words to Ana "No debo ir con ustedes . . .", and which the narrator archly suggests she might have over-interpreted (XIII, 284); the meeting of Ana and Mesía in chapter XVI (333), where no word of love is spoken, yet both are "convencidos de que por señas invisibles, por efluvios, por adivinación o como fuera, uno a otro se lo estaban diciendo todo"; amorous dialogues of the feet (XVI, 348-9; XXIV, 519); all the conversations between Ana and De Pas (most notably, XXIII, 503-4); the seduction of Petra (XXVII, 579-81). There is a contrast in almost every conversation between words and thoughts, between the appearances and the reality of communication. De Pas is particularly aware of this contrast, and he exploits it, bringing an extra sophistication to hypocrisy: realizing that his words are going to be reinterpreted, he plants, by implication or gesture, an extra-verbal meaning, which often has as little to do with the truth as the words themselves. Thus in a conversation with Carraspique's wife, he states that she should give money to various religious causes, while implying that if he were rich, like her, he would give generously; an implication that she duly catches and responds to (XII, 229). The ironical truth lies beneath the two levels of language and deliberate implication: it is that this sort of extortion in the name of the Church is precisely what has made him rich! De Pas has acquired, then, not only the "costumbre de dominarse y disimular" (XII, 242), which he shares with most of the other characters, but also the ability to handle the more subtle ploy of pretending to pretend; a motif taken up in a description of minor characters, the girls from Madrid who "fingían disimular su desprecio de todo lo que les rodeaba" (XXIV, 511: Ronzal plays the same game, XXX, 657). Effective communication takes place, it seems, through all channels but that of language; so that when, in times of crisis, a character most needs to confide in someone close to him, as De Pas does after hearing about Ana's fainting in Mesía's arms, he finds that he cannot (XXV, 523: see also XXX, 649-50). The critique of language that is built into *La Regenta* is but one of many fascinating aspects of the novel that critics seem not to have noticed; it might even be of passing interest to linguisticians.

Of all the characters in the novel, only the "failures" Camoirán, Guimarán and Quintanar – and Ana, in moments of abandon –

are usually sincere, stating directly in words what they mean. Hypocrisy is the rule in Vetusta; sincerity may bring its private rewards, but its practical and immediate consequence for the individual in this world of machiavellian scheming is only to leave him at the mercy of his rapacious fellows, to be pitilessly abused and exploited by them.

Spirit/matter

The characters in *La Regenta* are caught up in an oppressively material world; when some of them, in their search for fulfilment, attempt to escape from their material circumstances, or at least to assert the independence of their spirit from matter, they find that they cannot. Matter is an inescapable fact of their existence, and it is not to be denied. Weber (9) has shown how Ana and De Pas divide themselves into two parts, body and soul, which they like to believe they can keep apart (Ana XVI, 339, 353; XIX, 408; De Pas XVIII, 387; XXII, 474; XXV, 527; XXX, 646-7). But they cannot: the division is really little more than their attempt to justify some of the less worthy aspects of their behaviour. For, it is implied, there is no fixed frontier between the realms of matter and spirit, and no such frontier can be created, however hard the characters may try. The demands of the body intrude constantly: Ana's longing for spiritual fulfilment cannot be dissociated from her unsatisfied sexual needs; and her mystical feelings always occur when she is weak, convalescing after illness, the degrading physical aspects of which are stressed (XIX, 395; XXI, 440; XXV, 529). Other importunate interventions of bodily requirements are found in minor characters on a lower, grotesque level. There is Saturnino Bermúdez, with his "sonrisa llena de arrugas, que equivalía a una mueca provocada por un dolor intestinal, aquella con que Bermúdez quería pasar por el hombre más espiritual de Vetusta" (I, 24); Quintanar, who, faced with the sudden revelation about his wife's adultery, wants nothing so much as to return to his warm bed and go to sleep (XXIX, 630-3); and the country landowner who, visiting Vetusta cathedral, struggles "por contener impulsos del estómago cuya expansión hubiera sido una irreverencia" (II, 45). The congregation punctuates the Bishop's beautifully eloquent

Holy Week sermons with "los sollozos indispensables de los días de Pasión, los mismos que exhalaban ante un sermón de cura de aldea, mitad suspiros, mitad eructos de la vigilia" (XXII, 237); the cathedral is complete with "las inmundicias de cierto gato que, no se sabía cómo, entraba en la catedral y lo profanaba todo" (I, 23).

The depiction of man in *La Regenta* is not, however, a simple naturalistic or deterministic one in which all thoughts, feelings and actions are seen as the direct consequence of physical processes. Spirit is, in fact, no more to be denied than matter. Even though the events of the latter part of the novel seem to confirm the doctor's positivistic dictum "Ubi irritatio ibi flexus", an analysis of those events indicates this to be an oversimplification, as I shall attempt to show in my discussion of the novel's story later (pp. 52-5). There is not a straightforward one-way process, but rather a constant interpenetration of the physical and the immaterial, which also informs the text's many inner monologues, discussed below (pp. 37-41; see also Ife [20]).

Spirit/matter, then, like control/abandon but unlike sincerity/ hypocrisy and fulfilment/frustration, is presented in *La Regenta* as a dialectic rather than as a simple dichotomy. But it is a dialectic going, as it were, through the stage of antithesis: at the moment – that is to say, in the novel's present – matter appears to have the upper hand over spirit: "¡las cosas grandes, las ideas puras y bellas, andaban confundidas con la prosa y la maldad, y no había modo de separarlas!" (XVI, 324). The debasement of the spiritual by the material has taken place particularly in three areas, which correspond to the directions in which Ana and other characters look in vain for fulfilment: the Christian religion has been converted into cold, empty ritual; human love has become lust; culture is now little more than an excuse for snobbery. Let us look at each of these topics (or "sub-themes", as we might call them) in turn.

Religion/ritual. Weber has examined this sub-theme in her two articles (*8* and *9*). As she points out, most of the novel's action takes place on important feast-days in the Christian calendar, and it is full of scenes from Vetusta's corporate religious life, in none of which do the thoughts of those present, except Camoirán and occasionally Ana, even momentarily turn to religious subjects. They coldly follow the forms and rituals of religious observance while their attention is focused on quite different concerns, usually vicariously erotic ones. A climax of hypocritical nastiness is reached in the Easter procession in chapter XXVI, where all looks are for Ana, and "Cristo tendido en su lecho, bajo cristales, su Madre de negro, atravesada por siete espadas, que venía detrás, no merecían la atención del pueblo devoto" (XXVI, 554). The thoughts that the sight of Ana's naked feet arouse in the minds of those present, especially Obdulia, are coloured by a peculiarly unpleasant and perverse sexuality; Ana is aware of all this, and considers that she is "prostituting herself" (XXVI, 558; XXVII, 569). The Christian faith is vitiated at every turn, often in surprising ways : Mesía, in planning his final assault on Ana's virtue, does so in terms of the Christian calendar and its likely effects on her mentality and constitution (XXV, 531). The narrator frequently uses religious terms in ironically inappropriate contexts : "Visita era el papa de aquel dogma antirromántico" (XVI, 327); Mesía's drunken revelations about intimate details of his love life are described as a "confesión, que oían sus amigos con silencio de iglesia" (XX, 429), and the scene is reminiscent, "por modo miserable", of Leonardo da Vinci's *Last Supper*.

The sub-theme of the debasement of religion is embodied especially in De Pas. His efficient management of the diocese to serve his own and his mother's ends is set against the simple, genuine faith of the early Church (XII, 249); and his positivistic reduction of the Christian message to a mechanical question of "medicina" and "higiene" (IX, 167; XII, 239; XVII, 359) is contrasted with the Bishop's spontaneous exaltation in the beauty of the word of God. Even when De Pas, under Ana's influence, attempts to recover his faith, the confusion between matter and spirit besets both of them constantly, though often without their realizing it. He misdirects his fervour, thinking of Ana as a *madonna* (XXII, 472), and an *ángel* (XXII, 474), just as she refers to him as a *santo* and *mártir*. The height of confusion is reached when Ana decides to "sacrifice herself" for De Pas, in the procession on whose erotic content I have just commented; she envisages herself as Mary at the feet of the martyr Christ (XXIV, 506; XXV, 537; XXVI, 553). When the feelings that De Pas insists on believing spiritual and pure reach their most intense pitch, after he receives Ana's soulful letter in chapter XXI, the reality about those feelings is made plain to the reader, but not to De Pas, as, in the subsequent catechism scene, he dreamily caresses the girls upon whose "precoces turgencias" and "los misterios fisiológicos por que estaban pasando" the narrator dwells with malicious innocence. He finally turns back into the same worldly priest as he had been before coming into contact with Ana.

In spite of all this, *La Regenta* is not, of course, an anti-clerical novel; the Roman Catholic Church is not, as such, attacked in it. On the contrary, what its author considers to be the true values of that Church, as embodied in Bishop Camoirán, are implicitly defended against the corrupting influences of modern times.

Love/lust. As I have just observed, this sub-theme and that of religion/ritual interact continuously, since scenes depicting Christian rites – masses, processions, confessions, catechisms – are full of covert but intense erotic feeling. Both sub-themes are firmly established in the novel's opening two chapters, before, in the next three, Ana herself is introduced. With the description of first Celedonio and then, at some length, Saturnino, eroticism is presented at its most sordid and most ridiculous; conflicts which beset the major characters are reflected, in a grotesque form, in minor characters, an important aspect of the technique of this novel to which Weber (9) has drawn attention, and which I have already mentioned in other places in this chapter. The reader is implicitly invited to remember that, however subtle and sophisticated the erotic-religious feeling between De Pas and Ana may become, it is, in essence, no different from that experienced for Obdulia by poor Saturno. The minor characters, used as it were as distorting mirrors for the major characters, have the effect of degrading and belittling the latter whose conflicts, kept in such a humiliating perspective, are never allowed to attain noble proportions : *La Regenta* presents a comic, not a tragic, vision of life.

In the minor characters a wide range of sexuality is presented: as well as the pathetic Saturno and the perverse Celedonio, there is the devious and effeminate Don Custodio; the frivolous Obdulia; Visita, the volunteer go-between who aids Mesía solely for the pleasure of seeing Ana seduced; the *beata* Doña Petronila, a kind of procuress for the clergy; the young Ana's governess, Doña Camila, whose "pasión principal era la lujuria, satisfecha a la inglesa" (IV, 66); her aunts, frustrated spinsters salivating as they dwell on the details of the child's supposed sexual experience (V, 86); Teresina, characterized by her own peculiar mixture of false piety and vulgar sexiness from the very moment of her entry into the novel "abrochando los corchetes más altos de su hábito negro (de los Dolores)" (XI, 208-9); Petra, with her vicious sexual envy, jealousy and spite; Paco Vegallana, with his strange romantic idealization of the most basic libidinous urges (especially VII, 136-7); his father, for whom the winter cold acts as an aphrodisiac (XVIII, 376); Doña Paula, who has reached her present position by allowing herself to be seduced at opportune moments.

In the midst of a society composed of such elements, poor Ana's chances of surviving unscathed are indeed slim. After a childhood complete with its sexual trauma, the night on the boat with Germán (III, 54; IV, 69-71), she finds herself with a husband "incapaz de fumar un puro entero y de querer por entero a una mujer", as she muses at the beginning of chapter XVI, contemplating Víctor's half-finished cigar and converting it into a phallic symbol. She is introduced in a scene of intense frustrated eroticism (III, 50). And, after a long resistance, she finally surrenders to Mesía's campaign, in which the sordid predominates from beginning to end. Ana, enjoying at last some sort of satisfaction, is unaware that Mesía has never seen her as other than a desirable body to be possessed; that he is feeling his age, and has had to impose on himself a period of intense physical preparation in order to be sure of performing adequately when the moment of truth arrived; that, in order to enjoy Ana undisturbed, he has persuaded Petra to stand guard each night, and has seduced her, too, in order to ensure her loyalty. Ana does not enjoy her adulterous relationship for long. Her final symbolic punishment for it is to suffer a sexual attack, in the cathedral.

De Pas, as I have indicated, is no more capable than Ana of keeping lust away from love. True religious love has at least one representative in the novel; true human love has not even that. Base, loveless eroticism, on the other hand, pervades the world of *La Regenta*; it is the more squalid for being furtive and, indeed, often voyeuristic. The narrator's use of indirect language to refer to sexual subjects, whatever its causes, only adds to the general sense of devious unhealthiness, and so contributes positively to the elaboration in the text of this sub-theme.

Culture/snobbery. Saturnino Bermúdez also introduces this sub-theme in the first two chapters; his guided tour of the cathedral embodies, then, all three sub-themes of spirit/matter, and the considerable space devoted to its description in detail can thus be explained. Saturnino is the representative in Vetusta of learning, as Trifón Cármenes is the representative of creative writing. Each illustrates one aspect of the degradation of cultural values: Saturnino, with his pompous rhetoric, his pretentious provincialism, and his abject efforts to ingratiate himself with the aristocracy; Trifón, with his mechanical repetition of all the tired commonplaces of Romantic literature, and his unfailing stupidity and tastelessness. Yet, as Durand (6) and Brent (21) have shown, the degradation of culture, especially literary culture, is to be found on all sides in Vetusta. Pretentiousness, combined with ignorance, reduces literature to the level of any other stratagem in the struggle for social status, and cutting irony is directed by the narrator against it: Somoza "jamás había leído a Voltaire, pero le admiraba tanto como le aborrecía Glocester, el Arcediano, que no lo había leído tampoco" (XII, 223). The characters' frequent misuse of foreign, especially Latin, expressions, is treated with similar irony. Even a character who, like Víctor, is capable of a personal response to literature is, as the narrator is careful to demonstrate, wrong in his approach: literature provides for him, as it does to a less intense degree for other characters, an artificial world of bright colours and strong emotions into which to retreat momentarily from everyday life. It fails to provide any answers to the problems of the real world, even when, as in Víctor's case, the problems faced (adultery, cuckoldry) are the central concern of the literature read (the honour dramas of the seventeenth century).

Ana, unlike most of the other characters, has read and understood books, and she does not convert literature into mere snobbery or escapism. She has, when younger, even written poetry, for which Vetusta has duly ridiculed her. As Brent (*21*) has indicated, literature is for her something that must be intimately relevant to life, and she variously attempts to apply Pascal, Santa Teresa and Zorrilla (a curious mixture indeed) directly to her own experience. But she is hardly more successful than her husband; her elation during the performance of *Don Juan Tenorio* is no more durable that that which Víctor experiences during his private recitals of Calderón; and she is just as unrealistic as is he in imagining that parallels between the theatre and life can be valid. Again we see how the problems of a major character are reflected, in grotesque forms, in a minor character.

Literature by itself, it seems, can at best provide a temporary panacea. *La Regenta* thus appears as a doubly self-doubting text: it contains a searching critique not only, as I indicated earlier, of language, but also of literature itself.

I have tried to indicate how the principal themes of *La Regenta* are patterned in its characters, both minor and major. The wide range of these themes and the complexity of their patterning are, arguably, characteristics of the realistic novel. Rather than representing single concepts, each character, even minor ones, assembles and interrelates many themes in a special permutation: caricature, in other words, is avoided (caricature could be tentatively defined, in the terms of this analysis, as the drastic reduction of the number of main themes and the total polarization of those pairs of opposite concepts involved, so that characters are simple magnifications of single concepts). The relationships between characters, too, are complex: they are so frequently marked by an ambivalent combination of attraction and repulsion, of admiration and envy, that some such pair of opposites could almost be postulated as a fifth major theme. Mesía is Ronzal's "aborrecido y admirado modelo" (XVI, 345); Petra and

Teresina are good friends who "se respetaban sin perjuicio de
tenerse envidia" (XI, 213); Visita wants to see Mesía succeed in
seducing Ana, yet she is pleased to see him defeated and humil-
iated (XVI, 326-7); Víctor is full of petty malicious envy towards
his bosom friend Frígilis (XIX, 401); Don Custudio hates and
envies De Pas, but he dreams of future triumphs for him, and
although De Pas in turn despises Custodio, the latter serves his
purpose, for "la envidia de aquel pobre clérigo le servía para ver,
como en un espejo, los propios méritos" (I, 22). There is similar
ambivalence in the relation between De Pas and his mother, and
in Ana's feelings for Mesía; and there is a distorted reflection of
the latter in Saturno's wilful courting of sexual temptation as he
makes his extraordinary trips to Vetusta's red-light district
(I, 25-6).

Each character in *La Regenta* can, I have argued, be usefully
seen as a particular grouping of four main themes; each can be
defined, in other words, in terms of its various positions on the
axes control/abandon, fulfilment/frustration, sincerity/hypocrisy,
and spirit/matter. What we have in the text itself bears, of course,
little resemblance to any schematic model of this sort. The actual
characterization as it is presented to readers can be regarded as an
expansion and elaboration of such basic material. By this, of
course, I do not want to suggest that, while writing, the novelist
consciously carried out such a process: the analysis of an entity
and the history of its creation are two quite different things. The
manner in which the patterns of abstract themes are actualized
in the text is a question of what I have called narrative mode.

Narrative mode

In *La Regenta*, two aspects of narrative mode seem to be particularly concerned with characterization: the point of view from
which descriptions of characters are made, and their moral definition. Both are subjects which have been extensively and profitably
discussed in recent novel criticism, most notably perhaps in
Wayne Booth's *The Rhetoric of Fiction* (Chicago, 1961).

Point of view. Perhaps the most obvious and straightforward
way in which characters can be described in a narrative text is

from the standpoint of an omniscient narrator who presents each protagonist at the point where he first intervenes in the story, giving a summary of his relevant antecedents and physical and mental features; the characters are ushered in, one by one, each with, as it were, a label in his hand giving vital information. Few traditional children's tales depart very far from this model in its most basic, and scarcely elaborated or expanded form. Most writers of serious fiction for adults, however, have found this method excessively mechanical and repetitive, and have looked for other methods that offer more variety and greater expressive possibilities. The "label" can be handled in a more sophisticated way; or, alternatively, the character can be allowed to reveal himself, in the course of the action, through his words and deeds; or descriptions can be provided by other characters; or the narrator can use his omniscience to project the reader into the sensibility of a character, and give direct access to his most intimate thoughts and feelings about others and about himself. In *La Regenta* extensive use is made of all four methods; its technique for character presentation is both extensive and intensive, making possible both minute detail and broad panoramic views.

The "label", the most direct method of presentation, is used in *La Regenta* principally for the description of characters' physical features, which are, in turn, nearly always made, implicitly or explicitly, to indicate features of their personality. I have already said that eyes are given much attention, as an almost platonic reflection of the soul; similar processes are at work, though less insistently, in the description of other parts of the physique, and particularly the physiognomy (see, for example, the presentations of De Pas on I, 12 and of Custodio on I, 22). *La Regenta* is not, of course, in any sense original in its use of this technique. Labels are also used in *La Regenta* for the description of characters' antecedents and personalities. We need look no further than the presentation of De Pas for an example (I, 13: "Uno de los recreos . . ."; see also Don Cayetano, II, 34, and Pompeyo Guimarán, XX, 410). All of chapter IV, and most of chapter V, are taken up by a passage in which the narrator stops the story and summarizes, in some detail, the personality and past history of Ana; this, too, is a label, albeit a very lengthy one. A somewhat different type of label (IX, 177-9) gives the narrator's survey of Mesía's assessment of himself.

The process of self-revelation is virtually inevitable in any narrative work. As soon as an action, statement or thought of a personage is reported, some information is bound to come through, more or less indirectly, about that personage's make-up. Actions are normally, of course, more directly relevant to story than to characterization, but not always: the description of telling details of conduct plays an important part in the technique of characterization by self-revelation. The Marqués de Vegallana's habit of starting meals with an enormous dish of sardines, while others eat delicate hors d'oeuvres, then leaving the room and returning a little later to the soup pale and sweating, brings new refinements to the theme of degradation and perversion, as elaborated in the Marqués with his gross and inappropriately plebeian gastronomic and sexual tastes (XIII, 270: fresh sardines, eaten fried, are, in northern Spain, a cheap everyday dish, greasy and strong in flavour and smell, which would never normally appear at an aristocratic table).

The indirect delineation of character through the opinions of others is a technique much employed in *La Regenta*. It is important, for example, in the presentation of Camoirán (XII, 231-41). The opinions about him that are reported come from sources that the reader very well knows to be unreliable, and he consequently reinterprets these opinions: when, for example, he reads of the comparison that their congregation makes between the sermons of De Pas and the Bishop, preferring those of the former because he is better looking and has a more studied and elegant style (XII, 234), he remembers how incapable the Vetustans are of appreciating Christian virtues and understands that the truth is that the Bishop speaks with deep sincerity in contrast with De Pas, with his calculated rhetorical effects. The presentation of Frígilis through others' opinions has, as I have already indicated, a more ambivalent effect. In the case of the Bishop, the witnesses are totally unreliable; so the process of reinterpretation involves little more than the simple reversal of value judgments: Vetusta considers Camoirán far inferior to De Pas, therefore he is really far superior. There are, in addition, several judgments expressed directly by the narrator, to remove any possible doubt from the reader's mind. It is, however, much more difficult to determine exactly how reliable or unreliable are the other characters' opinions about Frígilis; and, in the virtual absence of any direct interventions by the narrator, he develops into a much more elusive and ambivalent character, as I have indicated.

A method much used for introducing characters' opinions into the narrative is illustrated in the following description of winter meetings round the fire in the Marquesa's sitting-room: "A su calor no se contaban *antiguas consejas*, como presumía Trifón Cármenes que había de suceder por fuerza en todo *hogar señorial*, pero se murmuraba del mundo entero, se inventaban calumnias nuevas y se amaba con toda la franqueza prosaica y sensual que, según Bermúdez, 'era la característica del presente momento histórico, desnudo de toda presea ideal y poética' " (XVIII, 376). The use by the narrator of his characters' expressions instead of his own serves several purposes. It makes it possible for characters to be introduced into the narrative, together with their foibles as reflected in their style of speech, in sections that have nothing to do with them; so that even when the narrative focusses on a small area of the novel's world, the sense of a society composed of a large number of variously interrelated individuals is retained. Thus both Cármenes and Bermúdez are kept in the reader's mind in a passage describing a *tertulia* which they are not privileged to attend. The device is full of latent irony, for the quoting of a character's pet expressions in this way implies critical comment: "Obdulia se acercó al dignísimo Pedro y sonriendo le metió en la boca la misma cucharilla que ella acababa de tocar con sus labios de rubí (este rubí es del cocinero)" (VIII, 153). Two other effects can be discerned in this sentence. The narrator implicitly mocks the chef Pedro's use of the commonplace "rubí", and hence also the glib donjuanesque insincerity that lies behind it; but by mocking the cliché he is able himself to use it and make it meaningful again: "rubí" thus also tells the reader something about Obdulia's cheap, superficial attractiveness. We may also notice that the narrator delays informing the reader that the expression is not his own until after he has used it: the reader consequently finds that he has, suddenly and unexpectedly, to

alter his interpretation in accordance with the new context into
which the expression is thrown, as the description that had
seemed to come from the omniscient narrator turns out, in fact,
to have come from one of his highly fallible characters. Other
examples of this sudden ironical change of perspective abound:
". . . el Rector del Seminario, hombre excesivamente timorato,
según frase de la Marquesa de Vegallana . . ." (XIV, 287); "La
novena de los Dolores tuvo aquel año en Vetusta una impor-
tancia excepcional, si se ha de creer lo que decía *El Lábaro*"
(XXV, 535).

The indirect presentation of a character, through other characters' opinions, offers further expressive possibilities. When we
read of A's opinion about B we are given, in synthesis, information about three separate things: A, B, and the relationship between the two; the device thus makes it possible for the narrator
to say several things at once. It also keeps the reader in mind of
the gossip that incessantly bounces back and forth within the
small, enclosed world of Vetusta. More than any other narrative
technique, perhaps, it enables the novel to have a broad scope
without presenting a simplified or generalized view of life.
Society, in *La Regenta,* is no anonymous mass but rather a large
number of individuals interrelated in complex ways; and so the
crowd is never presented as one unit, but rather as a collection of
different characters each with his own distinct actions and
thoughts (see particularly the scenes of Ana in the boulevard in
chapter IX, Paco Vegallana's party in chapter XIII, the dinner for
Pompeyo in chapter XX, Christmas Mass in chapter XXIII, and
the ball and dinner at the Casino in chapter XXIV). The device of
indirect presentation suggests, furthermore, the idea that any iden-
tity is a function of its context, that is to say of its position in a
network of interpersonal relationships; man is, then, a social
animal interacting constantly with his fellows, rather than an
isolated, independent individual. And characters often show themselves acutely aware of others' opinions about them, appraise
those opinions, and try to adjust their behaviour accordingly. We
are thus given not only A's opinions about B, but the repercus-
sion, with still more expressive and synthesizing possibilities, B's
opinions about A's opinions about B: thus Doña Paula com-

ments to her son about the gossip in Vetusta about them (XI, 215-17); Mesía imagines what Ana must be thinking about him (XVI, 328); and there is also, for example, De Pas's view of Ana's view of De Pas (XVI, 331), Mesía's view of Vetusta's view of Mesía and De Pas compared (XX, 423), and De Pas's comparison of his view of himself with his view of Vetusta's view of him (XXI, 449).

As in the last two examples, contrasts and comparisons often complicate and enrich the presentation of characters' opinions. When Ana assesses the relative merits of De Pas and Mesía (XIII, 265), she reveals much not only about the two men but also about herself; for although she believes her feelings towards them to be quite different, in fact she compares them in precisely the same terms of virile attractiveness. The narrator often draws up comparisons between different characters' visions of the same phenomenon. During their conversation on XXII, 474-5, Ana and De Pas have, separately, become finally aware of the force of their hitherto sublimated or submerged sexual feelings, but each fears to confide in the other. The comparison of their views of the situation produces strong irony; Ana's sweetness to him has aroused De Pas's sexual urges to an irresistible pitch, and he has had recourse to Teresa in order to satisfy them; yet Ana interprets his resultant pallor as a consequence of saintly studies and sacrifices, and behaves still more affectionately. During the period they seem to be closest, each is hiding from the other precisely the same secret about himself; each takes the other for a saint as he realizes most fully what a sinner he himself is. This type of symmetry is not infrequent in *La Regenta* (see also, for example, the confrontation between Mesía and De Pas, XXV, 531-2, and the morning of the Easter procession, XXVI, 553).

The other method of characterization I want to discuss here is that of sustained projection into a personage. The examples of projection I have so far referred to have been brief ones, occupying a few sentences at the most, where a character's private opinions about another are revealed. There are other passages in the novel where the narration is taken over, as it were, for quite long periods by one of the characters, into whose sensibility the reader is thus absorbed : passages of "inner monologue". I have

shown how characters can be described from a standpoint outside the world of the novel – that of the narrator, in labels; how
they can be described from a closer position, that of other characters in the novel, in opinions; the most internal form of description of all is that which a character gives of himself, in projections.

The first important projection in the novel occupies most of
chapter III, where Ana is presented as she thinks back over her
past; it is followed by the extended label of chapter IV and much
of chapter V, which adds some more information about Ana and
elaborates on some details, but also substantially repeats much of
what was said in chapter III. The difference in viewpoint does
not seem, in fact, to add anything new : the reader's reactions, for
example, to the incident in the boat as related by Ana (III, 52-5)
and by the narrator (IV, 69-71) are virtually identical. One possible reason for this repetition is the ambiguity that, as I have
already pointed out, pervades every account given by the characters, all of whom are to some degree unreliable. Chapter III
alone does not indicate to what extent Ana's memory is accurate,
and to what extent it contains a subsequent reshaping of events.
Ana is characteristically aware of this possibility : "La Regenta
recordaba todo esto como va escrito, incluso el diálogo; pero creía
que, en rigor, de lo que se acordaba no era de las palabras mis-
mas, sino de posterior recuerdo en que la niña había animado y
puesto en forma de novela los sucesos de aquella noche" (III, 54).
Ana does not, then, remember past events directly; she rather
remembers – as she believes, at least – a subsequent memory of
them, and an embellished and reordered, or novelized, memory
at that. We are thus at three removes from the events;
and things are complicated still further in the conversation with
Germán (III, 53), where the description of events from her past
has gone through four stages of processing and reprocessing :
events ﹥conversation in which Ana described them to Germán
(1) ﹥her later memory of that conversation(2) ﹥her subsequent
novelization of that memory (3) ﹥her present memory of all this
(4). At each one of these four stages she might have distorted the
account; the narrator, for the moment, refrains from comment-
ing, leaving the reader with the ambiguous "La Regenta . . .
creía que . . .". Thus it could be that chapters IV and V serve the

function of removing the ambiguity and confirming that, after all, the account given in chapter III is accurate. But then, of course, the question suggests itself why the ambiguity was created in the first place only to be very soon removed. It could be felt (to venture a passing critical suggestion) that this long section, occupying the larger part of two chapters, is one of the few places in this novel – I would argue that it is the only place – where much is redundant and whose removal would have done no harm to the work as a whole.

The projection in chapter III is highly expressive: that is to say that during it many things are expressed and implied simultaneously in synthesis. As well as being given an account of relevant aspects of Ana's past, the reader is told about her present situation and state of mind; largely in an indirect way, in the selection she makes of past events and the relative importance she attaches to them, in her interpretation and ordering of them, and so on. The ordering is particularly relevant: the device of the inner monologue makes possible an escape from chronological time, and an arrangement of events in more subtle and telling ways, for example by association of ideas. In other passages there is projection into characters who are making an assessment of their present situation, which is thus revealed in a more direct way. These passages are frequent in *La Regenta*, with its self-conscious characters; the narrator often presses into service the well-known device of the mirror, whose reflection of their physical aspect leads characters to meditations about their inner selves (XI, 211; XVI, 340; XXIII, 500-3; XXX, 650).

In contrast with labels, which tend to summarize, order and define the world of the novel from an outside, non-involved viewpoint, a projection gives the reader the illusion of being absorbed into the sensibility of a character, and of experiencing life with him, through his senses. Thus when Ana, left alone after everyone has gone to the theatre, involuntarily begins to weep, the reader is at first not told as much; her visual sensations are described, and the cause of those sensations – her tears – is defined only at the point where Ana herself realizes what is happening to her, and so is capable of defining it: "Miró al cielo, a la luz grande que tenía enfrente, sin saber lo que miraba; sintió

en los ojos un polvo de claridad argentina, hilo de plata que
bajaba desde lo alto a sus ojos, como telas de araña; las lágrimas
refractaban así los rayos de la luna. '¿Por qué lloraba?' " (X, 186).
Similarly when Víctor sees Mesía climbing out of his wife's bed-
room window (XXIX, 629-30), there is, at first, no direct description of his reaction, but rather a minute account of Mesía's
movements as they register on the retina of Víctor, numbed, as
the reader implies, by the unexpected horror of it all. His sense of
shock is conveyed, from the inside, all the more powerfully for
not being named. The language a character uses to describe
things – his own private narrative mode, as it were – is frequently reproduced : Ana's memory of her childhood is given in the
simple language of a child (III, 53); her sense of being caught up
in the plastic beauty of the countryside is conveyed by a long,
meandering sentence (XIX, 403-4); her inexpressible intimate
contentment at the return of her health is reflected in stammer-
ing, ungrammatical language (XXI, 454); her feelings as she
faints during the ball at the Casino are similarly paralleled by the
style of their description (XXIV, 520); short, staccato sentences
convey De Pas's turmoil after the disruption of his relationship
with Ana (XXV, 527).

The inner monologues of *La Regenta* possess several other
features in common, techniques used in nearly all of them in
order to give a sense of life experienced rather than defined.
Above all, perhaps, there is the constant interaction between the
inner and the outer worlds, between a character's thoughts and
feelings and his perception of "reality". Characters are never
isolated in their own musings for long; their thoughts are punctuated and redirected by the outside world as, through one sense
or another, it makes its constant presence felt. Inner monologues
are, indeed, often triggered by such perceptions of material reality. Ana, for example, after her first confession with De Pas,
walks into the countryside, where the birds that she first hears,
and then sees, lead her to find parallels in her own life for their
behaviour : she, like them, is dissatisfied with the shadows and
wants to fly high in search of better things (IX, 165-6). On
another occasion, immediately before her seduction, Ana's brief
but intense musings on her own state are set under way by

Visita's piano playing (XXVIII, 607). And once an inner monologue has started, thoughts are continually interrupted by the
outside world, and take new directions as a result. Ana, having
started late at night a self-examination in preparation for her
coming confession with De Pas, gets into bed and automatically
caresses a sheet, a habit which originated in her childhood as a
substitute for maternal caresses; the touch of the sheet thus sends
her thoughts suddenly back to that childhood, and away from
the confession (III, 50-1). This is a fortuitous interruption from
outside; often, however, their thoughts lead characters consciously to look to the reality surrounding them, as they project their
problems on to it and search for symbolic confirmation of their
feelings and ideas. Ana's inner monologue on All Saints' Day
(XVI, 323-6, 331-2) contains several examples of this process: the
damp, gloomy weather, the monotonous cathedral bells, her
husband's half-finished cigar, the complacent inanities published
in the local newspaper, the ill-concealed indifference of all Vetusta
towards the spiritual significance of the day, all are made quite
consciously by Ana into symbols of her personal plight (I shall
discuss symbolism further in the chapter on setting). And just as
the outside world can initiate inner monologues and direct their
subsequent course, so also can it conclude them. De Pas, having
entertained thoughts of a spectacularly bloody revenge after
learning about Ana's adultery, is brought back down to earth by
the fortuitous interruption of the sounds of his mother's moving
about upstairs (XXX, 650); Ana, sitting alone in the countryside
absorbed in her thoughts about flying in search of fulfilment,
suddenly feels the cold of late afternoon and so returns to reality
(IX, 170); she is even more abruptly taken out of her inner monologue when, wandering alone through her house, she is caught in
one of her husband's fox-traps (X, 187).

   Trains of thought thus proceed not steadily but in fits and
starts, by sudden, irrational yet explicable associations, as a mind
jumps from inside to outside, and from one moment in time, past,
present or future, to another. Much thought can often be synthesized in this way in a few words of the text, as in the culmina-
tion to De Pas's inner monologue which closes chapter XV (322).
The perception of the outer world takes place here through hear-

ing and sight; all the senses are in fact brought into play in these projections, especially in moments of elation, such as those experienced by De Pas after receiving Ana's letter (XXI, 442-50), and by Ana as she makes her decision to appear in the Easter procession (XXV, 533-8). The use of the senses is not only extensive but also intensive, as can particularly be seen in the frequent use throughout the novel of the device of the transposition of senses, sometimes known as synaesthesia: "un hombre de carne y hueso que tenía en la voz un calor suave y en las letras silbante música, y miel en palabras y movimientos" (XIII, 265) describes sound in terms of touch, then sound and sight in terms of taste; "varias canciones que caían de arriba como lluvia de flores frescas" (XXV, 536) is an apparently simple yet intense simile which fuses sound, touch, smell and sight; "Y don Alvaro sonreía de un modo que lo decía todo perfectamente, y hasta con acompañamiento de una música dulcísima que la Regenta creía oír dentro de sus entrañas" (XXVIII, 595) describes what Ana sees in terms of sound, which in turn is sensed not in the organ of hearing but in a part of the body where normally the only sensation would be that of touch; in another passage, which I quote a few lines later (XXI, 454), Ana's sense of taste is transposed to her *entrañas*. It will be noticed that each of these examples of synaesthesia describes, as do many others in the text, the perception of the hypersensitive Ana; each, furthermore, involves a reference to music, which plays a prominent part in many scenes.

There is also an effect of synaesthesia in the frequent attribution in *La Regenta* of physical sensations to the soul and other predominantly nonphysical components of human beings, especially again Ana. She "sentía cardos en el alma" (III, 55: see also XXV, 533); the soul is in other places invaded by *lluvia* (IX, 181), *perfume* (X, 193; XII, 234), *cosquillas* (XX, 412), *cieno* (XXV, 525), and *hielo* (XXVI, 558), the brain by *amargor* (XIX, 397; XXX, 646) and *migajas* (XXVII, 571), the heart by *brasa* (XIX, 397), the pride by *pinchazos* (XVI, 327). Occasionally Ana makes efforts to locate the seat of her emotions and sensations with greater precision: "Sentía, medio dormida, a la hora de amanecer sobre todo, palpitaciones de las entrañas que eran agradable cosquilleo; otras veces, como si por sus venas corriese arroyo de leche y miel, se le figuraba que el sentido del gusto, de un gusto exquisito, intenso, se le había trasladado al pecho, más abajo, mejor, no sabía dónde, no era en el estómago, era claro, pero tampoco en el corazón, era en el medio" (XXI, 454); "¡Bendito Dios!, las dulzuras que le pasaban por el alma, las mieles que gustaba su corazón, o algo que tenía un poco más abajo, más hacia el medio de su cuerpo" (XXIII, 496); ". . . la sensación fue más suave, más corrosiva. Ana la sintió llegar como una corriente fría y vibrante a sus entrañas, más abajo del pecho" (XXIV, 515); "Ana sentía un placer *puramente material*, pensaba ella, en aquel sitio de sus entrañas que no era el vientre ni el corazón, sino en el medio" (XXVIII, 598). Although Ana considers the pleasure to be "purely material", it is interesting to see that the exact place in her *entrañas* where she locates it is halfway between her heart (a common symbol of spiritual life) and her stomach or belly (which represent many of the most fundamentally physical aspects of existence) : in another expression of Ana's, it is "lo más suyo, algo que sería cuerpo que parecía alma, según era íntimo" (XIX, 395). The word *entrañas* is used on many other occasions to refer to characters' inmost being; it seems virtually synonymous in this text with *alma* (see, for example, VIII, 147; XVI, 329; XXIII, 503; XXV, 532; XXVIII, 606; XXIX, 626).

All the extended inner monologues belong to Ana and De Pas, with one exception : the passage in which Quintanar finds out about his wife's adultery (XXIX, 627-39). The conventional term "inner monologue" is, in fact, somewhat misleading when applied to passages in *La Regenta* of sustained projection; for what we more often have is a dialogue, or to employ a term I have already used with reference to other aspects of the novel, dialectic, between an individual sensibility and outside reality And so, as Weber (9) has pointed out, one of the text's themes is reinforced : never is it possible for spirit (thought and feeling, the individual's intimate inner self) to be kept apart from matter (his perception through his physical sensations of outside reality). The world of the mind cannot be isolated from the world of phenomena; one constantly invades the other. The real problem is, which invades which? Is spirit paramount over matter, or does matter govern spirit? But I have already suggested the characteristically complex answer that is implied in *La Regenta* : neither is paramount, for we have to do with a two-way process : sometimes the outer world imposes itself on the imagination (with its fortu- itous interruptions), sometimes the imagination imposes itself on the outer world (with its creation of symbols).

There is here, too, an illustration of a principle that underlies the techniques of character presentation in this novel. Individual characters are scarcely ever seen in isolation; the context – human, material, temporal – in which they are presented, and with which they incessantly interact, is everything. *La Regenta* gives an intensely organic vision of existence, as Ife (20) has clearly shown.

Moral definition. The actualization of characters in novels in- volves not just the elaboration of a permutation of themes, by techniques such as those I have examined, but also the assign- ment of a certain moral status to each individual grouping, that is each character. This judgment may be given directly or in- directly, and it may be rigid or leave room for considerable ambi- guity; but, as Wayne Booth has shown, no narrative text is free from it. All novels are, to begin with, created in the context of a certain culture, and so a whole body of assumptions is inevitably written into them : the reader needs no assistance from the nar- rator to assign a low moral status in *La Regenta* to the character who seduces, then abandons, his friend's wife. The function of literature is not only, however, to reproduce, illustrate and help to perpetuate cultural conventions, but also to subject them to critical examination. So although any individual text may be expected to conform to the broad outlines of its own culture, it may also be expected, within these limits, to make its own depar- tures; just as it must use a certain language and conform general- ly to its given structure, but at the same time may use this lan- guage in a more or less idiosyncratic way, creating as it were its own individual language system, or idiolect. So although narrator and reader can take some moral standards for granted, others, especially those which are original and variant, have to be individ- ually established in the text. That Mesía is a bad sort is fairly obvious; but to turn Bishop Camoirán's passivity, weakness and ineffectiveness into the positive qualities of an ideal Christian needs, as I have indicated above, special intervention by the narrator. And Frígilis, as we have also already seen, is a character whose moral status remains undefined, because neither are there external, generally accepted rules of conduct which he either upholds or contravenes in any obvious way, nor does the narrator formulate any clear judgment about him.

Textual judgments can be either implied or directly stated. Both methods are employed in *La Regenta*. Direct judgments are quite frequent; they are often sweeping, and assign moral status in an absolute way; and they are normally used to condemn. Hence the description of De Pas's office : "Los empleados tenían la palidez de la abstinencia y la contemplación, pero producido por los miasmas del covachuelismo, miserable, sórdido y malsano, complicado aquí con la ictericia de los rapavelas . . . Era una oficina como otra cualquiera, con algo menos de malos modos y con poco más de hipocresía impasible y cruel" (XII, 249). Such interventions are intended to define in clear terms, to remove all possible doubt or ambiguity. That is the intention; but sometimes in *La Regenta* the characters seem to escape, as it were, from their creator's grasp and from his attempts to define and delimit them, and to belie his directly stated judgments. The narrator loses very few opportunities, for example, to condemn Mesía, and he takes pains to show him to be not only wicked, but stupid and totally wrong in his assessment of situations; to reduce him, it might be said, to the infrahuman status of many of the characters in Alas's *cuentos*. Yet the fact, unpalatable though it may be for the narrator, is that the cynical and materialistic Mesía is more often than not quite right in his judgments. His way of thinking about Ana – in terms of her "cuarto de hora" (XVI, 334), her "impulsos sensuales" (XX, 421), her "misticismo erótico" (XXIV, 518), her "carne flaca" (XXIV, 519), her "locura" (XXVI, 558), her "pasión vehemente" (XXVIII, 605), her "hambre atrasada" (XXIX, 615), her "escrúpulos místicos" (XXIX, 616), and her "escrúpulos de aquella adúltera primeriza" (XXIX, 619) – is certainly just as outrageously *grosero* as the narrator insists; but that does not, unfortunately, prevent it from being accurate. The narrator might protest, for example, "no había tal cuarto de hora"

(XVI, 334); but when Ana herself has just informed the reader "Si ese hombre no viniese a caballo, y pudiera subir, y se arrojara a mis pies, en este instante me vencía" (XVI, 333), his protest is unconvincing. And of all the characters in the novel, only Mesía and the equally cynical and materialistic Petra and Doña Paula are successful in achieving in the end what they set out to achieve. The action of the novel shows Mesía to be right and the narrator to be wrong. And the technique that is intended to curtail the text's ambiguity in fact increases it; for the narrator's opinions are shown, in certain cases, to be just as unreliable as those of the characters. An authoritarian procedure turns out, in other words, to have subversive consequences, for the status of the entire text is thus laid open to question : if it is not controlled by its creator, then who is in control of it? Some, going to the other extreme, would allege that the reader is.

There are several different ways in which judgments may be implied in a narrative text. Descriptions are scarcely ever solely descriptive; the terms in which they are couched often imply an attitude. In *La Regenta*, for example, a description in terms of lack of warmth, colour or light usually implies a negative attitude, a point I shall return to in the chapter on setting.

The way in which the narrator normally implies judgments about his characters in *La Regenta* is, however, through the irony that pervades the novel. Irony in this text can be defined as the reduction of a character's moral status by implicit mockery and ridicule, as the reader is tacitly invited to compare and contrast what the character really is or does either with some excessively flattering opinion about him (often his own), or with what he should be or do, or with both. The real confronts, on one hand, the illusory, and on the other the ideal; the contrast is drawn up in such unfavourable terms that no explicit judgment is necessary for the character concerned to appear ridiculous. Let us look at some concrete examples.

The rich and complex irony of the conversation between Ana and De Pas which I have already discussed (above, p. 34) depends upon a multiple comparison, between what a relationship between a priest and a member of his flock should be like, the truth about the particular relationship between De Pas and Ana (to which only narrator and reader have access), and the beliefs about it of the two characters involved, each of whom is now acutely aware of the unpleasant truth about himself and yet totally mistaken about the other. The immediate juxtaposition of these various contrasting views carries its own implicit comments about the characters, especially about the willingness of each to continue deceiving himself about the other. Other examples of what we could call "irony of situation" are the conversation between Ana and Mesía (IX, 179-82), in which the frequent shifting from one viewpoint to the other is designed to reveal how wide of the mark is his assessment of her mental state; the similar scene in which the two are together in the theatre (XVI, especially 347-9); the finding by Víctor and De Pas of Ana's garter (XXVIII, 589-91); and Ana's requests to her husband and De Pas for permission to go to the ball at the Casino (XXIV, 507-10).

Dramatic irony similarly depends upon the contrast between the complete awareness of narrator and reader of what is happening in the novel and the partial ignorance of a character, who innocently says (or does) something that, in the light of the true facts of the situation, means or implies (or results in) something completely different from, and usually more sinister than, what he intended. In *La Regenta* it is the least damning type of irony, in that the reader is not invited to mock characters at whom it is directed, as is usually the case with the irony of this novel; he rather comes to sympathize with them for their innocence in a cruel and malicious world. Quintanar is the principal target of dramatic irony as, in his efforts to make his wife happy, he unwittingly does everything within his power to ensure that Mesía's plans to seduce her will succeed; dramatic irony accumulates about him in chapters XXVIII and XXIX, and it is, indeed, Mesía's exasperated appreciation of this irony that pushes him to take the final decisive step and seduce Ana (XXVIII, 609). Characters often share with narrator and reader the extra knowledge which loads another's statement with dramatic irony. When, at the Vivero, at the beginning of the storm, Ripamilán tells De Pas not to worry about Ana and the others since they must have gone to the woodchopper's hut and therefore be safe (XXVII, 586), De Pas, in possession of more information — not only about Ana's relationship with Mesía, but also about the hut's associations, for he has just seduced Petra there – interprets the statement as implying the precise opposite: Ana is in danger, from Mesía's advances. In fact the irony is more harmful to De Pas than to Ripamilán, as it emphasizes his excessive concern for Ana and thus helps to expose him to the ridicule which builds up rapidly during the next few pages.

The ironic contrast between the truth about a character and another much more indulgent view often takes the form of antiphrasis, the statement by the narrator of what, as he is careful to indicate, is the opposite of the truth. A simple example of antiphrasis is to be found in the description of the renewal, after the summer holidays, of the campaign of gossip against De Pas: "Todos ardían en el santo entusiasmo de la maledicencia" (XXII, 467). A set expression is turned on its head: it is clear that an enthusiasm for slander must, in any circumstances, be the very opposite of "holy"; though it is implied that the enthusiasm is so widespread and infectious that an innocent and idealistic observer might be forgiven for believing that it was for a worthy cause. Another example of antiphrasis is the description of the Vetustans' behaviour in the theatre: "No es mucho más atento ni impresionable el resto del público ilustrado de la culta capital" (XVI, 337). The general context of the novel as a whole and the immediate context of the theatre scene make it clear that this public is really the reverse of *ilustrado* and the city the opposite of *culta*. This example of antiphrasis is, however, somewhat different, and more characteristic of this text; for the ironical adjectives here implicitly represent the opinion not of a hypothetical outside observer but of the very characters they describe: Vetustans like to think themselves enlightened and cultured, although the narrator and reader know better. In fact antiphrasis is not essential to irony. In the novel's first sentence, for example, it is implied that the inhabitants of Vetusta presumptuously believe their city to be important and heroical, just because of its allegedly heroical past; the text immediately and ironically makes it clear that Vetusta is no longer at all heroical: for, to begin with, heroes are not caught having their afternoon nap, especially at the beginning of narratives. Vetusta is not, however, particularly cowardly;

the relationship between the narrator's view and the subject's view is one not of opposition but simply of negation.

Other descriptions in which this type of irony may be studied are those of Don Robustiano (XII, 223), of the "venerables canónigos" (II, 33; XVII, 356), of Doña Petronila and her *beatas* (XVIII, 377; XXIII, 504), and of Don Saturno, "contemplando su brazo extendido y su energía" (XXII, 479) and venturing into high society (XXIV, 512-13). In each of these examples the terms of the description correspond to the view of the subject himself, which is exposed by the contrast, on the one hand, with the implied view of the narrator and, on the other, with what is understood to be appropriate in such a situation. In the latter description of Don Saturno, for example, the irony depends on a sustained mock-heroic metaphor : the notion of swimming or navigating in a vast ocean is a gross and incongruous exaggeration of the difficulties Saturno has to face and conquer on entering the aristocratic salon. It corresponds to his view of the situation, the hyperbole is his; from the viewpoint of narrator and reader it is a pseudo-hyperbole, for its function in the text is not to impress the reader with Saturno's bravery, but on the contrary to expose to mockery his excessive anxiety to please and his consequent overdramatization of his dilemma. As usual, there is a double opposition : the real is contrasted at the same time with the illusory (Saturno's view of his role) and with the ideal (the sort of behaviour that would be appropriate in these circumstances).

The speech or thoughts as well as the actions of characters may, of course, be exposed to irony in a similar way. Often the contrast between the "truth" and what lies behind a character's words, or between what would be fitting and what he actually says, is so great that no comment from the narrator is necessary in order to point it out: the words in question only have to be marked in some way to make them stand out from their context and attract the reader's critical attention. The device of instantaneous quotation (see above, pp. 32-3) often has this effect. Italics frequently serve a similar purpose : see, for example, Mesía's (XVI, 348) and Obdulia's (XXI, 454) thoughts about Ana. A character's repeated use of a certain word or type of word, like Robustiano's "la ciencia" and Pompeyo's recourse to religious terminology, can have a similar ironical effect. Or the narrator may summarize a character's speech or thoughts in such a way that their absurdity is, as it were, concentrated, as in the reports of Don Frutos's speech about religious beliefs (XX, 432-3) and of Víctor's thoughts on the same subject (XXI, 457), and in the summary of Cármenes's article on All Saints' Day (XVI, 324). A way in which the narrator can seize upon a word used in speech by a character and expose it to ridicule is by repeating it subsequently in his own narration, as if it were his own word, and allowing the new context to show it up. In a conversation between Ana and De Pas (XXIV, 507) their new closeness is reflected in their use, in place of *usted*, of the first person plural, a kind of tentative semi-*tuteo*. The use in the immediately ensuing narration of the incongruous and ungrammatical *"fuéramos"* instead of "fuera" draws the reader's attention to the implications of this form of address : its unpleasant conspiratorial overtones, the dangers involved in the intimate relationship between Ana and her confessor. A similar effect can be observed in Víctor and "hipogrifo" (XVI, 335) and "santo varón" (XXVIII, 587), and the transparent euphemism "hablar" used by De Pas and Petra, then repeated by the narrator as a comic pseudo-euphemism (XXVII, 581).

In other passages the narrator adds some comment to a character's words or thoughts in order to ensure that the reader does not miss the implied contrast upon which irony depends. The comment frequently takes the form of an explanation which depends on a nonsensical proposition, and which thus highlights the fatuousness of the character in question; a form of *reductio ad absurdum,* the logic of which is frequently as tenuous as is that of many other literary devices : " – No es de fe – repetía [Quintanar] –, en mi opinión, creer que ese fuego es físico, material; es un símbolo, el símbolo del remordimiento./Algo le tranquilizaba la idea de que le tostasen con símbolos en el caso desesperado de no salvarse" (XXI, 457); ". . . aquel rincón aristocrático, elegante, donde se reunían los *hombres de mundo* (en Vetusta el mundo se andaba pronto)" (XVI, 341); "El Magistral sintió entonces impulsos de arrojarse de la torre. Lo hubiera hecho a estar seguro de volar sin inconveniente" (XVIII, 383-4); "En cuanto al 'elemento devoto de Vetusta' – frase de *El Lábaro* –, se metía en novenas así que el tiempo se metía en agua. El elemento devoto era todo el pueblo en llegando el mal tiempo" (XVIII, 376).

The method of summarizing a character's speech or thoughts known as *style indirect libre*, which I shall discuss in detail later (pp. 58-64), is full of possibilities for irony. It presents a report of a character's view of things which cannot be distinguished in any formal way from a description given from the narrator's viewpoint; and it is consequently a good vehicle for the reality/illusion opposition: "Don Alvaro estaba elocuente; no pedía nada, ni siquiera una respuesta; es más, lloraba, sin llorar por supuesto, 'de pura gratitud, sólo porque le oían'" (XXVIII, 597). Only the general tone of the passage, and the quotation marks surrounding the final seven words, indicate that the meaning is not "Don Alvaro asked for nothing, not even for a reply; what is more, he wept . . .", but "Don Alvaro said that he was asking for nothing. . . ." Thus the illusion (the former version, which Alvaro puts forth and which Ana accepts) is synthesized with its opposite, the reality, as narrator and reader are privileged to apprehend it. The contrast is reinforced by the apparent paradox "lloraba, sin llorar por supuesto"; not really a paradox, of course, since "lloraba" is part of the report in *style indirect libre* of Mesía's words, and "sin llorar por supuesto" is the deflating comment of the narrator. Here we may observe a common ironical process: the narrator momentarily seems to be taken in by the deceptive façades that his characters erect, and immediately shows that he has not been taken in at all. For the context belies what is stated, and enables the reader to reconstruct the implied truth of the situation (that is, the narrator's view of it), to contrast the two views, and so to form a hostile judgment about the character concerned. This process is worth detailed study, for it provides a good example of the working of literary competence: linguistic competence alone would not enable a reader to realize that, for example, "La heroica ciudad dormía la siesta" means, by implication and suggestion, very much more than it appears to say. An ironical narrator hides his malicious comment behind a cover of innocence, creating a significant interplay between the explicit meaning (which linguistic competence derives) and the contrasting implied meanings (which only literary competence gives access to). He is like the magpies so hated by Frígilis, who "con una especie de ironía . . . *fingían* estar descuidados, disimulaban su vigilancia . . ." (XXIX, 638).

In some passages the contrast between the real and the ideal is so great that irony can depend upon it alone, and the contrast between the real and the illusory is not necessary. In such passages (unlike those discussed so far) the character concerned may, consequently, become aware of the irony of his own situation; and if this happens, the irony is intensified. De Pas, in the scene at the Vivero during the thunderstorm, makes himself look foolish by behaving in a way quite inappropriate for a priest of some considerable social standing and prestige; and as he fully realizes the fact, yet is unable to alter it, so his ridicule is redoubled. It is De Pas himself who points to the irony of his situation just before his seduction of Petra : he contrasts his desire for Ana, whom he can never possess and whom he desires all the more urgently precisely because he can never possess her, with his lack of interest in the wretched Petra, whom he can have whenever he wants (XXVII, 581 : the reader will go on to contrast all of this with the ideal Roman Catholic priest, who desires no woman at all). Ana, too, brusquely brought down to earth from her dreams of fulfilment by getting caught in her husband's fox-trap – which was never any good at catching foxes – is all too aware of the irony of her situation, which is emphasized still more by the presence of the mocking Petra (X, 187-8). There are in *La Regenta* many other situations which principally depend for their irony on the contrast between what is fitting and what is : every one of the many scenes from Vetusta's public religious life, for example, embodies this type of ironical contrast. Play on the opposition between the real and the ideal is also behind the occasional use of literary parody in *La Regenta*. In the description of Mrs. Carraspique's tear (XII, 228-9), for example, there is parody of the sentimental novel, in which ladies weep tears in pairs. The irony is directed against the character rather than the style of writing : the ideal situation, as a certain type of literature presents it, is contrasted with what actually happens, at the expense of the dignity of the character concerned. Irony functions in the same

way in the description of Carraspique himself who "no se distinguía ni por su valor ni por sus dotes de gobierno : se distinguía
por sus millones" (XII, 222); here the parody is of the flattering
brief portraits of rich and powerful men to be found in some
history books and most obituaries. The narrator even parodies,
on occasions, the very style in which he is writing. The first description of a personage in a realistic novel is normally of a general
type, as the reader is given an overall impression of his appearance and character. In *La Regenta*, however, initial descriptions
sometimes depart radically from this norm, when the narrator
picks and dwells on some detail which is at the same time a
minor and an undignified part of the character concerned, but a
part which he nevertheless shows to typify the whole. So Visita
and Obdulia are memorably presented in terms of the comparative cleanliness of their underclothes (VIII, 150); Pompeyo
Guimarán in terms of his belly (XX, 410); Vetusta itself in terms
of the rubbish in its streets (I, 7).

I have tried in this section to indicate the different types of
irony to be found in *La Regenta* and to formulate the principles
underlying them all. There is one type of irony that I have not
yet mentioned, for it is the ultimate irony, that which is arguably
at the heart of the creative process : irony which the narrator,
unwittingly it seems, directs against himself. For is it not
supremely ironical – in other words, is there not a radical implicit
contrast between the narrator's illusions and the text's reality –
when the character that the narrator has taken the greatest pains
to prove wrong is shown to be quite right in his wretchedly
cynical assessment of the situation (above, pp. 42-3)? Might not
the moments of greatest creativity in a text come when it liberates
itself from its writer : when it writes itself?

The narrative mode of *La Regenta*, as it concerns characterization, is no simple collection of neutral mechanisms for actualizing themes, for in the very process of actualizing themes it reinforces them. Techniques are not, then, to be identified with the
concept of "form", as opposed to "content"; techniques have
implicit meanings of their own, and thus contribute directly to
the total vision of life presented in the novel.

In general terms, I would conclude that the function of the descriptive techniques in *La Regenta* is that of rounding out the basic theme-groupings that I suggested in the first part of this chapter to be the core of literary characterization : of giving them flesh and blood, as it were, and thus turning them into characters that the reader can be induced to accept and sympathize with as if they were real people. The function of the techniques of moral definition is to cast a highly critical light upon these characters and, with few exceptions, to make them look mean, ridiculous or wicked. The techniques of description – and especially those of projection, used in this text for all characters, even minor ones – tend to bring the characters close to the reader, by making him understand their motivation and their problems; the techniques of judgment tend, on the other hand, to distance or alienate the reader from the characters. Detailed description and projection thus counterbalance condemnation and satire. There is a continuing tension between the two opposing forces; so that the reader cannot either scornfully reject the characters, for he understands them too well, or identify with them, for their follies and sins are shown too clearly. He is led, rather, to the cheerless conclusion that all human beings, himself included, are puny and laughable creatures; so that to laugh at others – as we do, heartily, throughout *La Regenta* – is to laugh at ourselves. And so it is that, like two other Spanish masterpieces, *La Celestina* and *Don Quixote*, *La Regenta* is at the same time an uncommonly funny and a deeply serious book.

III. *Story*

The study of story focuses attention on what characters do rather than what they are; more specifically, what they do in order to bring about or prevent changes in situations in which they find themselves. A character who finds his situation undesirable can be expected to act to alter it, and one who finds his situation desirable will normally try to prevent any alteration. Thus all stories are based upon a dialectical process: first, a given situation; then, actual or prospective attempts to reverse it; and finally the new situation which emerges as a result of the conflict between the two forces. This new situation will be a repetition of the initial one if the modifying action is unsuccessful, or a reversal of ,it if the action is successful; and in turn it may be subject to new modifying actions. Any individual story is composed of one or more of these basic three-stage processes.

In *La Regenta* the story is far from being the centre of interest; for such a long novel comparatively little happens, especially in the first fifteen chapters, which are almost completely given over to character and setting. All the same *La Regenta* has a story, as, by definition, do all narrative texts. In the following brief analysis it will be remembered that I am talking about the events themselves, as the reader is expected to imagine that they "actually" happened, rather than the manner in which those events are described; the latter is a question of narrative mode as it affects story, which I shall discuss afterwards.

The novel's initial situation affects several characters, and for all of them it is an undesirable one. In particular, Ana is bored, frustrated, dissatisfied; Víctor is worried about his wife's listlessness; Mesía desires Ana, but has had as yet no chance to conquer her; De Pas feels that he deserves something more rewarding than his present situation can offer him, and he also comes, at first without realizing it, to desire Ana. All four characters try in different ways to change the situation to suit their needs; a protracted struggle, which occupies some nine-tenths of the book's length, finally results in Mesía's achieving, with the unwitting help of Víctor, precisely what he wanted, De Pas's failure to satisfy any of his diverse desires, and Ana's transient happiness in Mesía's arms. The adultery, in turn, creates an undesirable situation for Víctor which – according to the standards he has always maintained, those of the Golden Age theatre – can only be remedied by the drastic punishment of the erring lovers. After the plotting of De Pas and Petra has presented Víctor with evidence of his wife's infidelity, he finds Mesía in the sights of his shotgun, but he cannot bring himself to pull the trigger. De Pas's visit stirs Víctor into challenging Mesía to a duel, against Frígilis's advice; it results, however, not in the punishment of Mesía but in the death of Víctor. After her subsequent isolation Ana tries to regain contacts with the outside world by renewing her relationship with De Pas. His violent rejection of her is followed by Celedonio's repulsive kiss, her final degradation and punishment : a specifically sexual retribution for her sexual transgression.

The story of *La Regenta*, as I have attempted to abstract it, brings together some of the work's themes in different types of combinations from those I have outlined in my discussion of characterization.

The actions taken by characters in order to change situations in which they find themselves involve, principally, the theme control/abandon. Each individual process develops, as in all stories, in terms of cause and effect, for in each process the final situation must necessarily be a direct result of the modifying action or actions. In addition, the various processes of punishment which occupy *La Regenta*'s final two chapters grow inevitably out of the first process. In both these ways the story seems, in a sense, to be beyond the control of the characters, obeying inexorable and impersonal laws of logic rather than being directed by their efforts. Yet the factor of individual choice intervenes so decisively in the story of *La Regenta* that its causality is constantly being challenged. In none of the processes is the final situation reached as the immediate, planned result of machinations or intrigues, but rather as a consequence of a character's exercising his faculty of choice. Ana only falls into Mesía's arms after protracted fluctuation between him, De Pas and her husband; Mesía has, of course, always intended things to happen as they eventually do, yet the working of the story stresses that Ana always had a genuine choice, that the seduction is far from being a simple question of an intrigue leading to a predetermined conclusion. Intrigue now intervenes decisively, with the machinations of Petra and De Pas which bring about the dénouement. This is not, as it might superficially appear, an arbitrary, contrived climax of the "deus ex machina" type. From the point of view of the lovers the disruption of their relationship comes, indeed, as the result of an unexpected intrusion from outside; yet in the context of the novel as a whole, the plotting of the two coldly calculating characters, the jealous De Pas and the spiteful, envious, resentful Petra, is a perfectly logical development. At this point, then, the laws of logic rather than independent choice seem to be in command. Yet things do not work out at all as planned; for, ironically enough, Víctor – the character most pushed around by his circumstances – now resists the pressures on him and chooses not to behave as expected. He does nothing to his wife: punishment is avoided not, as is often the case in stories, because the ill-doer takes evasive action, but rather because the punisher does not want to punish. Víctor, too, has the other offender in the very sights of his gun; but instead of squeezing the trigger, with the inevitable consequence of Mesía's death, he prevaricates and finally chooses to challenge him to a duel – itself a situation of total choice. De Pas's sinister persuasion has been responsible in part for this decision, though the priest was planning for some more direct and certain form of revenge. But his plans are frustrated at every turn. Although, according to all logic, Víctor, the ardent hunter and excellent shot, should defeat Mesía, a novice with guns, without any difficulty, in fact Mesía kills Víctor; but only because the latter, in his compassion, chooses to aim for the other's legs instead of his body, and misses this much more difficult target. And Víctor, shot in the belly, only dies because he has failed to take the elementary precaution of emptying it before the duel. His death is, then, a result not of external forces over which he can have no influence but, on the contrary, of his own decisions; his fate was always, to this extent, within his own hands. And again, at the end of the novel, when Ana desires a reconciliation with De Pas, she goes about achieving it not by persuasion or intrigue, or other courses of action designed to stimulate the desired response in the other, but rather by suddenly going to him, and thus offering him a free choice between acceptance and rejection. Choice, then, is set up at every stage in the story of *La Regenta* against logic and causality. Choice is central to every modifying action in the story; causality is central to the very notion of story itself. The two opposing forces pervade the novel, which can be seen as a continuing, unresolved struggle, an unending dialectic between free-will and determinism.

The situations involved in the story of *La Regenta* principally concern the theme of fulfilment/frustration and the sub-theme of love/lust. Ana looks for something that will make life meaningful; she finds temporary sexual relief but, in the long term, only redoubled frustration and cruel punishment. The story of *La Regenta* is an account of man's blind, floundering search for fulfilment; in other words, his search for God – a God who seems cold, remote, uninterested, quite unconcerned to intervene in the search in order to give encouragement or guidance; but who is pitiless and implacable when this very search itself leads man astray. A bleak and depressing view of life, and one which it is not easy to countenance. Perhaps it is not surprising that *La Regenta* has failed to gain the reputation it deserves.

Narrative mode

Story is, then, an alternation of situations and forces undermining those situations. A "pure" story would read something like this : "Ana was spiritually and physically frustrated, and both Mesía and De Pas desired her; so Mesía plotted and planned, De Pas cultivated an ever closer relationship with her, and Ana finally chose the physical satisfaction that Mesía offered; with the result that Ana's frustration was temporarily relieved, Mesía achieved precisely what he wanted, and De Pas was thwarted. Now De Pas plotted with the servant Petra to put an end to the relationship between Ana and Mesía . . ." The "pure" story is, however, rarely found. Actions and situations are seldom sum-

marized so briefly, but rather are dramatized in more or less
detail; and the chronological time-sequence is not often so rigidly
adhered to. Narrative mode concerns the story of *La Regenta*
principally in these two ways: the manner and degree of expansion in the text of the basic situations and actions of which the
story is constructed, and their ordering: what I shall call, respectively, narrative speed and narrative sequence.

Narrative speed is a question of the relationship between the
time that things "actually" take to happen in the story and the
time that the narrator takes to relate them. If an incident is summarized in a few words, the narrative speed will be increased; if
it is dramatized in detail, the pace of the story will be reduced.
An extreme example of summary is ". . . a la hora señalada Anita
se presentó de rodillas ante la celosía del confesonario./Después
de la absolución . . ." (XVIII, 385-6), where only the events immediately preceding and following the action are referred to, and
the action itself occupies the space between the end of one paragraph and the beginning of the next. An extreme example of
dramatization is the description of De Pas's reliving of the events
which led him impetuously to visit Víctor, in the first moments of
the visit as he drinks a glass of water (XXX, 645-51); his thoughts
and feelings are reported in such detail that it might seem that
time stops, and indeed for the disturbed and confused De Pas,
caught for once with no idea of what to do or say, time does stop.

In general terms, the narrative speed of *La Regenta* increases
greatly in the second half: chapters I-XV occupy three days,
chapters XVI-XXX three years. The narrator uses the normal
realistic technique of a combination of the two manners; and,
logically enough, the important situations and actions are dramatized in considerable detail, and less central parts of the story are
summarized more or less rapidly. What is more particular to this
novel is the continuous alternation in it between the two manners,
an aspect of the restless, nervous changing of style which characterizes it. It is unusual for any single viewpoint or line of
approach to be adhered to for very long: all the different narrative
manners available to the narrator are brought together constantly

to interrupt, answer and reinforce each other. Thus passages of summary are usually enlivened by illustrative dramatized interruptions; and passages of dramatization are often punctuated by sections of summary which give brief explanations of facets of the action or situation described, or which hurry the reader through less relevant intermediate scenes. The two manners are thus intermingled; and although one necessarily dominates in any given passage, the other is rarely absent. Indeed the two are quite often fused, in the many scenes in *La Regenta* that are described in the close detail which corresponds to a dramatized account of a single event, yet with verbs not in the preterite but rather in the imperfect tense, which indicates a general summary of events that happened several times. The detail and the imperfects are logically incompatible: Mesía, for example, cannot have seduced all his many victims, like Angelina, after dinner on Christmas Eve (XX, 429-30). It is this sort of twisting of logic that literary competence enables us to accept and understand: we interpret a scene presented in this manner as having happened in precisely the way described only, of course, once, yet as being representative of many other similar occasions: Angelina becomes, for the moment, all of Mesía's victims. This manner of narration combines, then, the economy of summary with the liveliness and immediacy of dramatization. There are many other examples of it: Don Pompeyo's conversations in the Casino (XX, 412-15); the gossip in the cathedral (XX, 418-19); Ana's attempts to regain faith (XXV, 533-4).

The alternate acceleration and slowing of time that is produced by the use of summarizing and dramatizing passages can have its own expressive effects. Ana's seduction is preceded by a rapid summary of the activities at the Vivero which, during several months, prepare her for it (XXVIII, 606); and its very rapidity intensifies the sense of the giddy inexorability of her fall, once she has finally given up her attempts to resist the pressures on her to behave in the same lax and frivolous way as everyone else. A brief summary of an action can suggest, often ironically, that the action was performed in an unduly hasty or thoughtless way: "Ronzal fue desahuciado" (XII, 229) stresses how immediately and unquestioningly are accepted the recommendations of De

Pas and hence how powerful he is, just as "Pasó media hora. Sonó . . ." (XXV, 524) emphasizes the rapidity with which his commands are obeyed and his domination of Doña Petronila and Ana; and the summary style of the sentence starting "La Marquesa estuvo . . ." (XIX, 389) is itself an indication of the summary nature of the marchioness's visit. By making time pass in a flash, the narrator can create a telling juxtaposition of ironically contrasting situations: "Somoza dijo que aquello no era nada. Ocho días después propuso a la señora de Guimarán el arduo problema de lo que allí se llamaba 'la preparación del enfermo' " (XXVI, 541).

One aspect of reporting manner which deserves particular attention is the way of recording speech and thoughts. The two most used and most well-known ways are, of course, "direct speech" or "direct discourse" (abbreviated in the following pages as "DD"), which dramatizes the spoken or unspoken words, and "indirect speech" or "indirect discourse" (ID), which summarizes them. Extensive use is made of both in *La Regenta*. There is a third way of reporting speech and thoughts that was discovered by French critics earlier this century and named by them "style indirect libre", which could be translated as "free indirect discourse" (FID) – ID "freed" (that is, made syntactically independent) by the omission of the introductory subordinating nexus "he said that" (etc.). Thus the recording of Ana's thoughts which, in DD, might read "Estaba sola. –¿Adónde ha ido mi doncella? – se preguntó", and in ID "Estaba sola. Se preguntó adónde había ido su doncella", appears in the text (IX, 170) in FID: "Estaba sola. ¿Adónde había ido su doncella?" What might seem a trifling technical detail is well worthy of attention, as indeed are many aspects of narrative technique that still tend to be dismissed as trifling details. Its interest and importance spring from the fact that, unlike the other two reporting manners, FID is not formally marked. Linguistic competence alone would not enable a reader to understand the example of FID I have just quoted; he would, logically enough, consider the question to be a part of the continuing narration, and to be addressed, therefore, by the narrator to him. Only literary competence enables a reader to realize that this cannot be so, since such asides from narrator to reader are totally foreign to the narrative mode of this text; and that the question must consequently be seen as having been formulated by Ana.

FID offers many expressive possibilities. Above all, perhaps, it enables edited accounts of speeches or thoughts to be given without any of the remoteness and monotony that inevitably go with extended passages of ID. The omission of the subordinating nexus has the effect of disguising the narrator's intervention and bringing the reader closer to the character. A report in FID can, furthermore, keep closer to the style of the character concerned than can one in ID. ID summarizes the ideas of the character but its style is that of the narrator; DD reproduces the style of the character, word for word; FID ranges freely between the two extremes. It combines, in other words, the concision of ID with the sense of immediacy of DD; it is a type of dramatized summary, of what either one character or a group of characters thinks or says. In the latter case, we have a kind of "choral" FID: "Pocos meses después de la fiebre, Ana había crecido milagrosamente, sus formas habían tomado una amplitud armónica que tenía orgullosa a la nobleza vetustense. La verdad era que el tipo aristocrático no se perdía, pese a la chusma que no quería clases" (V, 90). And because reports in FID are totally unheralded, it is well suited for the rapid switching of viewpoint which, as I have indicated, is a central feature of *La Regenta*'s narrative mode. It is, in fact, much more often used in this novel for thoughts than for speech, which is normally reported in DD.

Since there is nothing in the linguistic form of FID to distinguish it from the narration in which it is embedded, it has to be signalled in some other fashion. A common type of signalling, used in the two examples I have quoted, is for either the style or the ideas of the passage in FID to be so out of consonance with those of the narrator, as they have been established in the text so far, that the reader is prevented from attributing it to him, and assigns it to the nearest character instead. It is not the style of this narrator to indulge in conspiratorial asides with his readers, and he has made it clear that he does not believe in the innate superiority of the aristocracy of Vetusta: therefore the expressions I have quoted are not his, but those of the characters nearest to hand,

Ana and the Vetustan aristocracy respectively. Similarly, in "[Quintanar] venía del teatro muerto de sueño – ¡no había dormido la noche anterior! – y lleno de entusiasmo liricodramático. Francamente, aquellos enternecimientos periódicos [de Ana] le parecían excesivos y molestos a la larga" (X, 193), the fact stated in the six words enclosed in exclamation marks cannot have any emotional significance for the narrator, but only for Víctor, with his petty bourgeois preoccupation with the details of his physical comfort; so the reader identifies it as a brief FID projection into Víctor's thoughts, rather than as a simple explanation by the narrator of the fact previously stated. It does explain that fact, but thanks to the insertion of something as apparently insignificant as a pair of exclamation marks it also adds a vivid detail to the characterization of Víctor. In the following sentence, the first word shows that we are back "inside" Víctor; it would be pointless for the narrator to say that he is speaking "frankly", for it is an essential part of the agreement implicitly entered into at the beginning of every novel by narrator and reader that the former, even though he is writing fiction, shall not knowingly tell lies.

FID cannot always, however, be signalled in this way. There is a basic ambiguity in it, which incidentally offers possibilities for irony, as I have commented above (p. 48). But often its ambiguity serves no useful purpose, and would only tend to cause unnecessary confusion for the reader. In *La Regenta* a formal sign is often used to eliminate purposeless ambiguity and to show that a passage is in FID: quotation marks enclose the passage in question. Strictly speaking, this procedure creates another type of discourse, whose title has, as far as I am aware, yet to be invented: "enclosed FID", perhaps. In *La Regenta* EFID is much more common than true FID.

One of the many examples is to be found at the crucial moment when Petra informs De Pas about Ana's adultery: "Petra le miró cara a cara, fingiendo humildad y miedo; 'quería ver el gesto que ponía aquel canónigo al saber que la señorona se la pegaba'./ 'Petra dijo, sin rodeos, que había visto ella, con sus propios ojos, lo que jamás hubiera creído . . .'" (XXIX, 624). The fact that the passage "quería . . . pegaba" is to be attributed to Petra would have been fairly clear without the quotation marks, for the brutal and vulgar style of the last five words is not the narrator's but hers; EFID does clarify, however, that the projection begins with "quería" and not "la señorona", as might otherwise have appeared. But the second pair of quotation marks throw the passage they enclose into a totally new and characteristically complex perspective. They show that it is not the narrator's summary in ID of Petra's key speech, but that it rather records the registering by the horrified De Pas of that speech; that, in other words, the narrative viewpoint has suddenly switched from Petra to De Pas. The quotation marks not only eliminate ambiguity about point of view but also give an impression of greater fidelity to the words spoken or thought by the character and thus, in the case of thoughts, intensify the sense of projection. Paradoxically they give this effect of immediacy as much when the words enclosed are a rapid summary in which the narrator's ironic presence is clear: "Petra volvió a llorar. '¿Cómo pagaría ella tal caridad, etcétera, etcétera?'" (XXIX, 626); as when they fully dramatize thoughts or speeches: "'Sí, él era como un eunuco enamorado . . .'" (XXIX, 625-6).

EFID serves other purposes. It can compress and hasten the narrative: "[De Pas] Llegó a la [casa] de doña Petronila Rianzares. 'La señora estaba en misa'" (XXV, 523) synthesizes "Llegó a la casa y llamó a la puerta. Contestó una criada a quien De Pas preguntó por doña Petronila. La criada respondió – La señora está en misa." An account in EFID of a character's thoughts is often juxtaposed ironically with his contrasting spoken words, given in DD: "Cuando [Víctor] le preguntaba si era él por su ventura el primer hombre a quien había querido, Ana inclinaba la cabeza y decía con una melancolía que le sonaba al marido a voluptuoso abandono: /– Sí, sí, el primero, el único. / 'No le amaba, no; pero procuraría amarle'" (V, 104). Quotation marks can be used to reinforce and lengthen the pause which is indicated by a full stop; and points in inner monologues where the train of thought comes to a halt, and then sets off in a new direction, are often thus marked: ". . . ocho días faltaban para la próxima confesión, ¿por qué había de venir? 'Porque sí, porque él lo necesitaba . . .'" (XVIII, 384). Ana's thoughts after her brief meeting with De Pas are similarly punctuated (XXIII, 500).

There are still more types of discourse in *La Regenta* than the
four I have discussed so far (ID, DD, FID, EFID). There are
occasional examples of what has, logically enough, been called
Direct Free Style, in my terms Free Direct Discourse. It has
approximately the same relationship with DD as has FID with
ID: in other words, it involves a passing straight from the narrative to a direct reproduction of a character's words, without
the transitional expression "he said, thought, etc . . ." (and without quotation marks or dashes): " '¿Qué serían, cómo serían en
adelante sus relaciones con Ana?' Don Fermín se estremecía. Por
de pronto mucha cautela. Tal vez el día en que dejé la puerta
abierta a los celos la asusté y por eso tardó en volver a buscarme.
'Cautela por ahora . . . , después . . . , ello dirá' " (XXVI, 559).
The first and last sentences are in EFID, the second is simple
narrative, and the two which follow it jump, without formal
indications of any sort, straight into De Pas's thoughts, reported
in FDD (though the third sentence, because of its lack of verbs
and personal pronouns, could also be in FID). The use of FDD
in fiction, especially pre-twentieth-century fiction, is rare; it
surprises, even jars the reader, partly because it is unusual and
therefore unexpected, partly because of the sudden grammatical
breaks it involves.

In *La Regenta* what I must call "enclosed FDD" is more common. The use of quotation marks has the effect of, as it were, soft-
ening FDD's blow on the reader's literary competence, and thus
making it more acceptable. EFDD is only distinguished from
DD by the omission of the transitional "he said" etc. (as well as
by the fact that the words reported are usually enclosed by quotation marks, not dashes). Yet the effect of EFDD is quite different
from that of DD. In particular, the "he said" of DD draws the
reader's attention to the mediating presence of the narrator; and
consequently its suppression brings the reader closer to the character, and fosters the illusion of immediacy – as also do the quotation marks, as I have already argued in my discussion of EFID.
Indeed, EFDD is arguably the sort of discourse which brings
reader and character closest together, for its defining features –
being freed, enclosed and dramatized – all independently have
this effect: "No dormía su marido. Se oía un runrún de palabras.

/'¿Con quién habla ese hombre?'" (XXIII, 501); "la esposa no resistió tanto como él esperaba; se rindió pronto. Pero él lo achacó a su propia energía. 'Comprende que yo no he de ceder y no se obstina'" (XXIV, 509). In many DD conversations the narrator does not, of course, add "he said" to every speech, and so some of the dramatic immediacy of EFDD can be obtained: "don Alvaro buscó más en lo oscuro . . . llegó al balcón entornado; lo abrió . . . /– ¡Ana! /– ¡Jesús!" (XXVIII, 609).

Finally, there are occasional experiments in *La Regenta* with various combinations of quotation marks and ID. The effect of EID is, of course, to indicate that the summary thus enclosed is close to the original; like FDD it is unusual and thus seems strange, even discordant, though in fact it is no more illogical than EFID, and occurs fairly frequently in *La Regenta*: "El coronel contestó 'que por Dios y todos los santos continuasen viviendo donde habían nacido . . .'" (IV, 65); "En voz baja decía el aya que 'la madre de Anita tal vez antes que modista había sido bailarina'" (IV, 67); "Los inteligentes opinaban que el prelado 'se había descompuesto'" (XII, 237).

If we look closely at the text of *La Regenta*, then, we find that the two or, at most, three styles into which the reporting of speech or thought is normally divided are hardly sufficient. The technical distinctions between the seven forms of discourse I have examined may appear to be small; but, as I have argued, each different form has its own quite individual expressive potential, and each functions in the text in a significantly distinct way, to vary the narrative speed and the distancing of the characters. Each type of discourse can be defined and distinguished from all other types in terms of three variable factors: whether it dramatizes or summarizes; whether it is syntactically independent or not; and whether it is marked by punctuation or not. I have argued that dramatization, syntactical independence and punctuation all reduce distance between character and reader, and that summary, syntactical dependence and lack of punctuation all increase it; so the various types of discourse can be seen as exploring the different intermediary zones between the close identification of EFDD (dramatized, independent, marked) and the distancing of ID (summarized, subordinated, unmarked).

The numerate will be asking about the eighth type of discourse (DD without dashes or quotation marks): there are a few examples of it in *La Regenta* (XX, 428; XXII, 474), but it is rare enough in this novel not to merit detailed attention here.

The narrative mode of *La Regenta* is characterized not only by the use of an extraordinarily wide range of reporting styles, but also by their constant intermixture. It is most unusual in this text for any single type of discourse to be adhered to for long. The lengthy speeches of Robustiano (XII, 226) and De Pas (XVII, 360), both reported throughout in DD, are exceptional; and so, although in other novels the manner of their reporting would carry no particular significance, here the impression is conveyed in both places that the character concerned is speaking with unusual eloquence and verve. Much more characteristic is the following brief passage, with its constant, dynamic varying of speed, distancing, viewpoint, discourse : "Cuando a Fortunato le ofrecieron el Obispado de Vetusta, él vaciló, mejor dicho se propuso pedir de rodillas que le dejaran en paz; pero Paula le amenazó con abandonarle. '¡Eso era absurdo!' Solo ya no podría vivir. 'No por usted, señor, por el chico es necesario aceptar.' / 'Acaso tenía razón.' Camoirán aceptó por el chico . . . y fueron todos a Vetusta" (XV, 314). In inner monologues, too, the sustained use of any one type of discourse is rare; the passage describing De Pas's feelings after Petra's revelations, in uninterrupted EFID (XXIX, 625-6) – which indicates how submerged he is in his own thoughts – is less characteristic than, for example, Mesía's inner monologue on XX, 420-1, in which the rapid succession of different types of discourse conveys an impression of nervous excitement and disturbance.

Narrative sequence. I have already referred (above, pp. 29-41) to the techniques used in *La Regenta* to present characters' antecedents, that is those events which occurred before the start of the story that are relevant to the depiction of the characters it involves; and I have pointed out how much use is made of shifts, often sudden ones, back and forth in time. Now I am concerned solely with the novel's present, the period occupied by the story itself : that is, the events and situations between Ana's initial coming to De Pas and Celedonio's kiss.

My singling out of the ordering of events as an important feature of narrative mode in *La Regenta* suggests that there is much disordering : if the objective chronological time sequence were followed throughout the telling of the story, there would be little point in dwelling on the fact. Actually the central thread of situations and acts is presented in the order of their occurrence; there is no major displacement of chronological time, such as characterizes much modern fiction. Here, as usual, *La Regenta* remains within the limits of realistic narrative technique, exploiting to the full all of its possibilities rather than initiating any radical innovations. But within the overall framework of the main story of a long novel like *La Regenta* there is plenty of room for the storyteller to manoeuvre. His most frequent manoeuvre is suddenly to jump forward in time, and then to relate the events of the period omitted not, therefore, as they happen, but rather as a character subsequently thinks back on them. De Pas's return home in the midst of a thunderstorm after the debacle at the Vivero is a brief example of the technique : " – ¡Eso!, ¡eso! – rugió mientras abría la portezuela y se apeaba frente a su casa – ¡Esto sólo se arregla con rayos! / Y entró en su casa después de pagar al cochero. / Los rayos que quería le esperaban arriba dispuestos a estallar sobre su cabeza. / Cuando se acostó aquella noche, pensaba que en su vida había tenido tan formidable reyerta con su señora madre" (XXVIII, 593). This passage relates several actions, but the three central ones are : (1) De Pas returns home, (2) he quarrels with his mother, (3) he goes to bed. The narration jumps, however, from (1) to (3) (though the way is smoothed by the transitional fourth sentence); and then (2) is reported retrospectively, from the vantage point of (3). Thus, while (1) and (3) are described from the external viewpoint of the narrator, the description of (2) comes from the character involved, De Pas.

The same type of temporal inversion occurs repeatedly in *La Regenta*, usually on a larger scale than in the example I have quoted. In chapters II and III, Ana and De Pas think about the coming confession; then, in chapters VIII and IX, the reader learns that the confession has taken place, and finds out about some of its details as Ana's thoughts about it are reported; and in chapter XI De Pas thinks back to the confession, and more details are given from his viewpoint. A later confession is handled in a similar way (XVIII, 385-8). With Víctor's death, the narration comes to a halt; as it reopens some five months have passed, and in the next section (XXX, 664-70) the events of the intervening period are related as they have affected Ana. These events themselves are not revealed in chronological order : there are, in other words, flashbacks within the flashback. First there is a rapid summary of Ana's illness and convalescence; then comes the scene, earlier still, of Frígilis's breaking to Ana the news of her husband's death; then her receipt of Mesía's letter; her illness, now dramatized from her viewpoint; her banishment by Vetusta; and finally back to Ana's present situation, the result of all the events just described.

The division of novels into chapters creates in them a series of formal breaks in narration, where abrupt changes in time or space can conveniently be made; and narrative inversion in *La Regenta* is most often associated with chapter endings. Chapter XVI starts, for example, nearly a month after the end of chapter XV; and, as Ana reflects on her situation and on recent events, so the intervening period is filled in. But although the flashback is initiated by Ana's musings (XVI, 323), the viewpoint soon changes, alternating between Visita, Mesía, De Pas and Ana herself in a characteristically rapid manner, until it finally returns to Ana and the narration is brought back to the present (XVI, 331). The effect is of a rapid 'round tour' of different views of the same events. Much is thus compressed into a few pages : here is yet another technique which combines the concision of summary with the liveliness of dramatization. In the second half of the novel, with its increased narrative speed, it is frequently used. Chapters XVII, XIX, XXVII, XXIX and XXX start with similar jumps forward in time, followed by flashbacks about the period omitted.

The technique of narrative inversion makes possible an escape from the objective, linear time sequence. It tends to shift attention away from story towards characterization, by connecting events with characters rather than with each other, and thus presenting them as being of interest not so much in themselves or as part of a developing story, but rather in their effects on the characters concerned. The indirect presentation of events through the consciousness of a character who looks back on them, is – like many of the techniques I have been discussing under the heading of "Narrative mode" – a synthesizing device; in other words, it makes possible the simultaneous conveying of information about several different things : the events themselves, their effects at the time on a character, their subsequent effects on him.

A similar technique, which seems to me to be more idiosyncratic, is that of narrative redoubling : an event is first reported from the viewpoint of an external observer, and subsequently described all over again, but now from the viewpoint of one of the characters immediately concerned, and usually in more detail. I have already mentioned one example of redoubling, where it is combined with inversion : Ana's illness after her husband's death is first rapidly summarized (XXX, 665), and a little later dramatized, from her viewpoint (XXX, 666-7). Redoubling often goes with inversion; another example is the expedition of Ana, Víctor, Frígilis and Mesía, first presented as a series of actions overlooked through his telescope from the cathedral tower by De Pas (XVIII, 383-4), and later described again, and now explained, from the viewpoint of Ana (XIX, 403-5). But redoubling can, of course, occur independently, as with the seduction of Doña Paula by Francisco de Pas (XV, 308), Mesía's appearance on a white horse (XVI, 332 and 334), his visit to Ana (XX, 437-8; XXI, 458), and the *Paulinas*'s attempt to gain access to Guimarán's deathbed (XXII, 477-80). In each of these examples the redoubling technique as I have outlined it is slightly varied : the seduction is first related not by an outside observer but by Doña Paula herself, 'n confession, but in a cursory and fairly detached way; the scene of the white horse is narrated on both occasions from Ana's viewpoint, the emphasis the first time being on the events themselves, and the second time on their emotional significance for her; Mesía's visit is described from his viewpoint initially – but then he is, on this occasion, the equivalent of an unknowing outside observer, as Ana's later narration shows; the affair of Don Pompeyo and the *Paulinas* is, on the other hand, described on both occasions from the standpoint of an external observer, the first time in rapid summary and the second in dramatized form. In spite of the individual variations the basic pattern is constant :

first a fairly neutral description of a series of actions; secondly, the "inside story" about them.

A similar effect is produced when the significance of an action or situation is only revealed some time after its description. De Pas, striding through the cathedral (I, 21-2), comes across "dos señoras" and "una joven pálida" and pays no particular attention to either. He, and the reader, only realize later (II, 39) that the former are Visita and Ana, who has come for confession; and much later (XV, 322) that the latter is Santos Barinaga's daughter, one of the agents of his enemy Don Custodio. There are similar delayed explanations of Víctor's religious preoccupations (XX, 436; XXI, 444), of Ana's letter to De Pas (XXI, 441; XXI, 442), and of the intimate behaviour of De Pas and Petra (XXI, 466; XXII, 475). In general terms, the effect of redoubling and delayed explanation is to divide the narration of an incident or situation into two separate stages: first, the action, and then the meaning of the action. As inversion is a synthesizing procedure, then, so redoubling and delayed explanation are analytical procedures. They separate and contrast external and internal views of events and also, more often than not, their apparent insignificance with their real relevance. They can have other functions. Ana's decision to perform an act of self-sacrifice for De Pas (XXV, 537; XXVI, 550) is another case of delayed explanation. Here, the explanation is withheld not only during the initial description but also on two subsequent occasions when it might well have been given: the conversation in which Ana tells De Pas about her decision (XXVI, 544) and De Pas's later thoughts about this conversation (XXVI, 545). Suspense and expectation develop as the reader awaits the revelation of the nature of Ana's self-sacrifice; and a powerful sense of climax accompanies Ana's appearance in the Easter procession, for the reader just as for Vetusta. The withholding from the reader of vital information and the consequent development of an enigma is a technique much used in narrative prose; it plays a minor role, however, in *La Regenta*.

The way in which the story, such as it is, of *La Regenta* is told is not a simple means to an end: it makes its own independent contribution to the total sense of the work. Indeed, it could well be argued that the storytelling technique of this novel is more important than its story – and the paradox is only apparent. My arguments in the previous pages have, in part, been intended to indicate that narrative technique is no mere question of dull, routine literary engineering, as most of those who attack the modern tendency in criticism to pay attention to technical matters appear to assume.

IV. *Setting*

The physical surroundings that are described in a narrative text and within which the characters live their imaginary lives usually play a subsidiary role. Since most novels are primarily about people, not places, the normal function of setting is to support characterization and story. In *La Regenta* it does so in various ways. As in any realistic novel, it provides an explicit grounding in material reality for the narrative, and hence enhances its sense of realism. Setting is, furthermore, at a rudimentary level, a cohering influence in *La Regenta*: Vetusta gives the novel unity of place, as Durand (5) has pointed out. But these two purposes of setting would be served by the description of a random selection of buildings in Vetusta. They alone cannot explain why certain features of townscape are described and given prominence in preference to all the other features that could have been included, but which are not mentioned or are only referred to in a summary way. For, although there is much detailed description of places in *La Regenta* (especially in the first half), this description is concentrated on quite a small number of areas; Brent (21) is wrong when he criticizes the novel for excessive and indiscriminate description of setting. I want to attempt to explain the selection of setting by returning to the basic notion of themes as the organizing core of a literary text, and by suggesting that themes that, as we have seen, are involved in complex combinations in character and story are reinforced by being projected into various chosen aspects of the setting.

Thus, to begin with, the theme matter/spirit is supported by the restriction of the novel's setting not only, in fact, to Vetusta but to the old aristocratic quarter of the city: this is where the characters, especially Ana, are caught, as if in a maze or a prison, claustrophobically hemmed in by the material reality of their surroundings, which help to make spiritual escape so difficult. There are occasional tantalizing glimpses of a more open, inviting world outside, and characters even get away occasionally into it: new, working-class Vetusta; the countryside around; the Vivero; local holiday resorts; Madrid. In particular, the environmental opposition country/town corresponds to the thematic opposition fulfilment/frustration. The countryside, with its clear sky, the majestic Corfín mountain, and its open fields, has a grandeur which makes Vetusta and the life of its inhabitants seem, by contrast, mean and petty. The hope of fulfilment seems to lie out there; but the characters are here, in Vetusta, and tied here (see especially XII, 250-1; XIV, 297; XVIII, 371-2; XXIX, 638). Ana's brief trips outside old Vetusta bring her temporary relief, a glimpse of *poesía*, as also does the performance of *Don Juan Tenorio*, brought to the city from outside by a travelling theatrical company; but she, like all characters except Mesía, is inexorably drawn back each time into the *prosa* of her home environment.

Yet even within the narrow confines of old Vetusta, there are many areas that are only briefly referred to. The reader is told comparatively little, for example, about the houses of two of the three principal characters, Ana and De Pas, and nothing at all about where Mesía lives. Detailed description is reserved for the public buildings in which most of the action takes place, each of which can be seen as an environmental representation of one of the three sub-themes of the matter/spirit theme.

The cathedral complex, described principally in the first two chapters, represents the perversion of religion and its transformation into empty, loveless ritual. Inside, the cathedral is gloomy, colourless and cold, as also are the Salesas convent (XII, 227) and San Isidro church (XII, 236-7). Outside, its beauty is a reminder of the spiritual strength of an earlier age, but modern illuminations debase it and turn its stately tower into a giant champagne bottle (I, 7-8). The cathedral dominates the novel. Even when the action moves away from it, the insistent chiming of its bells infiltrates its atmosphere into all Vetusta. The action starts there, with bell-ringers on the tower, and there it ends. Next to the cathedral, and permanently in its shadow, the Bishop's palace, described in chapter XII, is decrepit and dingy, and the offices it houses are dirty and cold; yet, in contrast, the Bishop's private rooms are colourful, happy and alive. The atmosphere of Doña

Petronila's house, a sort of annexe to the cathedral complex, is an unhealthy mixture of languid voluptuousness and pharisaical piety. It can easily be seen that buildings repeat the themes that are embodied in the characters that inhabit them.

The *casino*, described in chapters VI and VII, and the theatre, described in chapter XVI, together represent the perversion of culture and its transformation into ignorant snobbery, as Brent (*21*) has shown. Both buildings have seen better days and are now damp, draughty, and in an advanced state of decay.

The third sub-theme, the perversion of human love and its transformation into eroticism, is represented principally by the Vegallanas' palace and Vivero. These are, in practice, public buildings, since they are the focal points of the upper classes' frivolous social life. The palace, described principally in chapters VIII and XIII, is a place of flamboyant and decadent luxury, which reaches its height of bad taste in the *salón amarillo* and the Marquesa's adjacent sitting-room, where the seduction of Ana takes place. Much attention is also centred on the kitchen. The two principal activities in the palace are flirting and eating, both under the Marquesa's benevolent eye, and the two are linked and to some extent identified: banquets have the intense sensuousness of a Bacchanale about them, and conversely sexual activities are often referred to by narrator and characters in gastronomic terms. Visita's sweet-eating is explicitly described as a sex-substitute (VIII, 161). The kitchen, with its sumptuous array of rich food – seen (VIII, 151) as a collecting-house for all the edible flora and fauna in the province – is a centre of erotic activity. The chef is a philanderer, and he flirts with Obdulia as he prepares the food; he regards his job itself as a kind of culinary pandering, the very basis therefore of all the erotic horseplay that characterizes the palace (VIII, 153). The Vivero, a place of temporary refuge from the city, is the other centre for sexual amusements: the prepara- tion of Ana for her seduction takes place there. It is a fragile, artificial, escapist paradise (see Ana's description of it, XXVII, 574-5): the tender tranquillity enjoyed there by Ana and Víctor in chapter XXVII is doomed to come soon to an end. Although set in the country, it is in fact an extension of Vetusta, and no fulfilment is to be found there. The very last scene at the Vivero brings harsh reality to it: the duel and Víctor's death.

Narrative mode

Characterization, as I have tried to show, can be described as one system, and the ways in which characters are presented in the text as a different system, with its own principles. I have suggested that the same distinction is valid for story; and I am now going to suggest, as might be expected, that it is valid for setting as well.

Of the various techniques commonly employed in *La Regenta* for the description of setting, symbolism is probably the most important. I have already indicated (p. 38) how the characters often see aspects of their environment as symbolic reflections of their personal situation. The narrator, too, gives the environment symbolic meanings; such meanings are implicit in the very selection he makes of locations, as I have just suggested.

Most of the individual symbols belong in an overall system of symbolic values which run through the novel. The system is based on a simple dichotomy: the desirable and good – fulfilment, spiritual values, *poesía* – symbolized usually by light, warmth, agreeable sounds and perfumes; against the undesirable and base, symbolized by darkness, cold, dirt, damp, often slime. Thus, as we have already seen, the countryside is contrasted with Vetusta, the Bishop's rooms with the cathedral. Also, for example, spring and summer contrast with autumn and winter; the weather plays an important role throughout the novel, as both a cause and a symbol of characters' states of mind. Birds are on the positive side the equivalent of toads on the negative side. And a striving for heights stands opposed to a sinking into the depths of the earth. De Pas on the cathedral tower and in the pulpit at the beginning of the novel, Ana climbing a hill (IV, 78-9), even Mesía upon his white horse – at least in Ana's eyes – (XVI, 332-5) are all characters attempting in one way or another to raise themselves above the mediocrity of everyday Vetusta life, to fly high in search of "regiones superiores, llenas de luz" (XVI, 332), "una región de luz y calor" (XVI, 338), "luz, calor, espacio" (IX, 166). On the other hand, "pozo" (which can mean not only "well" but also "cesspit"), "agujero", "abismo", "charco", and associated words like "lodo", "fango", "inmundicias", "podredumbre", stand throughout for the fall back into the base material reality of the human condition, and, in particular, the reality of sexual desire. In this symbolic context, the fact that one of the favourite games of the young people at the Vivero consists of jumping on top of each other into a well (XVI, 327; XXVII, 581) acquires extra significance. The symbols of heights and depths are synthesized in the metaphor which is used to describe Ana's feelings for Mesía : "Se sentía caer en un abismo de flores. Aquello era caer, sí, pero *caer al cielo*" (XXVIII, 597). Thus clichés are given new life and meaning by being brought into the particular symbolic system of this text. The climax in *La Regenta* of negative symbolism is probably Ana's disturbing dream of an original and personal hell (XIX, 398); the fullest use of positive symbolism, De Pas's sense of being in a kind of heaven (XXI, 445-6, where the cathedral is, for once, described as a place of warmth and colour). That which is desirable is, then, represented by images that are intensely pleasing to the senses, and the undesirable by images that are unpleasant or even disgusting. The symbolic system of *La Regenta* makes, therefore, its own contribution to the spirit/matter theme : abstract notions which refer to the life of the spirit, such as *poesía*, *prosa*, fulfilment, frustration, and spirit and matter themselves, are often expressed in a form that is not only physical and material but also powerfully sensual. I have already commented (pp. 38-40) on the intensive and extensive use of the senses in the description of setting.

La Regenta is, of course, too large and complex a text for all its symbols to fit straightforwardly into such a scheme. There are important symbols that are not sensual at all. One is De Pas's clerical clothes, in particular his long cloak or *manteo*, an insistent and ambivalent symbol. On one hand, its majestic, ample, rhythmic flow stands for his elegance, energy, and superiority over all those around him; this symbolism is insisted upon in De Pas's presentation (I, 9, 10, 11, 21) and reappears frequently (XI, 212, 221; XII, 250; XV, 311; XX, 423). On the other hand, it represents, especially for De Pas himself, a negative aspect of his situation as a priest, the social and sexual isolation it involves;

and the notion of the man in skirts, with hints of castration and homosexuality, recurs (XIV, 290; XIX, 398; XX, 420; XXV, 527; XXVII, 578; XXVIII, 593; XXIX, 625; XXX, 646, 650). The negative symbolic values of *manteo* take over from its positive values in the course of the novel, as De Pas's frustration mounts : the two come together in the crucial scene of the swing (XIII, 281). Even within the system of sensual symbolism, the cathedral is, on one occasion, described in positive terms, as I have said; and nature is described in negative terms (XXIX, 635). On both occasions the exception is caused by the state of mind of the character whose impression of the setting is given : for De Pas, in a state of extreme elation, even the gloomy cathedral looks cheerful and bright, because he now chooses to pay attention to the few bright and cheerful features in it; and for Víctor, immediately after the revelation about his wife's adultery, even the countryside is a miserable and desolate place. This is, in a sense, a realistic explanation and adaptation of the Romantics' pathetic fallacy.

In spite of such exceptions, there is clearly a coherent symbolic system underlying the description of setting in *La Regenta*. Another process worth noticing is that of personification, or, more accurately, animation, since inanimate things – buildings, furniture, the countryside, the weather – as often acquire the characteristics of animals as of humans in this text. In the novel's first paragraph, the city is described as a person having his afternoon nap; the wind as *perezoso* (an animating adjective often used for the weather); the waste paper, straw and rags blowing about the streets are butterflies first, and then street urchins; and the wind, again, is given a will and an independent life of its own. Only, ironically, the people of Vetusta seem to lack life. Animation is a technique used throughout the novel. It gives the setting an extraordinary vitality, suggesting that it is not merely a passive background for human affairs but that it intervenes actively in them; and it thus reinforces the theme of the heaviness of material reality.

V. *Conclusion*

La Regenta is a text characterized by an extraordinarily full exploitation of the narrative resources of the nineteenth-century realistic novel. It is no experimental work; Galdós was the great experimenter of the period. Rather than attempting to break new ground, it uses and develops techniques and ideas already essayed by previous novelists, in particular Flaubert. Its style, as a result, is one of deceptively casual intensity. It is a novel that reads easily, that apparently demands of the reader no great efforts of comprehension. Yet the hidden, implied meanings, to which only literary competence gives access, are at almost every point of greater importance than what is actually stated – what, in other words, linguistic competence alone would enable us to understand. To put it another way, the language of *La Regenta* itself embodies that critique of language which is implicit in the descriptions of conversations in the novel (above, pp. 20-1). *La Regenta* is a plural text: one characterized, that is, by the simultaneous production in synthesis of several complementary meanings.

La Regenta is a remarkable novel. It is hard to comprehend how such a finished and complex piece of work could have been the author's first, and virtually his only, novel; even harder, perhaps, how its author could also have been the man who wrote all those dogmatic, facile *cuentos*. Yet it had no public or critical success when it was first published in 1884-5, and it has only been very recently – within the last five or six years – that it has begun to receive, in Spain, some of the attention it deserves. It is arguable that, as well as being too pessimistic to find ready public acceptance, it was just too good for its own times, that its subtle artistry quite simply escaped the public at which it was directed. An examination of its critical reception confirms this conjecture. To return to a concept I have employed frequently, the literary competence of the reading public was, in the 1880s in Spain, little advanced beyond linguistic competence. For the rebirth of a national literary tradition, after the long hiatus since the end of the Golden Age, was only just beginning, especially as far as the novel was concerned; the growing bourgeoisie was starting to learn to read and understand literature. Some ninety years later – and some eighty years after the embittered Clarín finally rejected as naive illusions his previous hopes that his toils in the creation of *La Regenta* might have resulted in something worthwhile – literate Spaniards are beginning to realize that they have a masterpiece on their hands. The film of *La Regenta* is even now being made.

Bibliographical note

For the historical background, (*1*) Raymond Carr's *Spain 1808-1939* (Oxford, 1966) is indispensable. An excellent recent work to consult on the general nineteenth-century Spanish literary background is (*2*) *A Literary History of Spain* (ed. R. O. Jones): *The Nineteenth Century*, by Donald L. Shaw (London, 1972). Pelican Books' forthcoming (*3*) *The Age of Realism*, edited by F. W. J. Hemmings, places Spanish realism in its European context. For a fuller discussion of the technical and theoretical aspects of the analysis of narrative texts, see my paper (*4*) "Character, Story, Setting and Narrative Mode in Galdós's *El amigo Manso*", which will appear in the symposium *Style and Structure in Literature* (ed. Roger Fowler).

Little of value has been written more specifically on Clarín and *La Regenta*. There are some useful articles, of which the most interesting are perhaps those by Frank Durand and Frances Weber. Durand's articles are (*5*) "Structural Unity in Leopoldo Alas' *La Regenta*", *Hispanic Review*, XXXI (1963), 324-35; (*6*) "Characterization in *La Regenta* : Point of View and Theme", *Bulletin of Hispanic Studies*, XLI (1964), 86-100; and (*7*) "Leopoldo Alas, 'Clarín' : Consistency of Outlook as Critic and Novelist", *Romanic Review*, LVI (1965), 37-49. Weber's articles are (*8*) "Ideology and Religious Parody in the Novels of Leopoldo Alas", *Bulletin of Hispanic Studies*, XLIII (1966), 197-208; and (*9*) "The Dynamics of Motif in Leopoldo Alas's *La Regenta*", *Romanic Review*, LVII (1966), 188-99. The articles by W. E. Bull, on (*10*) "The Naturalistic Theories of Leopoldo Alas", *PMLA*, LVII (1942) 536-51; (*11*) "The Liberalism of Leopoldo Alas", *Hispanic Review*, X (1942), 329-39; and (*12*) "Clarín's Literary Internationalism", *Hispanic Review*, XVI (1948), 321-34 are worth consulting, even though, as Sergio Beser shows in (*13*) *Leopoldo Alas, crítico literario* (Madrid, 1970), Bull pays inadequate attention to the radical aspects of Alas's thought in an attempt to make him appear a diehard reactionary. Sherman H. Eoff compares *La Regenta* with *Madame Bovary* in a chapter of his (*14*) *The Modern Spanish Novel* (New York, 1961), as also do Carlos Clavería in (*15*) "Flaubert y *La Regenta* de Clarín", *Hispanic Review*, X (1942), 116-25, G. Laffitte in (*16*) *"Madame Bovary* et *La Regenta*", *Bulletin Hispanique*, XLV (1943), 157-63, S. Melón Ruiz in (*17*) "Clarín y el Bovarysmo", *Archivum*, II (1952), 69-87, and Juan Ventura Agudiez in (*18*) "Emma Bovary-Ana Ozores o el símbolo del amor", *Romanic Review*, LIV (1963), 20-29 — none of them, however, very satisfactorily. Mariano Baquero Goyanes includes an article on (*19*) "Exaltación de lo vital en *La Regenta*" in his *Prosistas españoles contemporáneos* (Madrid, 1956, pp. 33-173). Barry W. Ife's recent article on (*20*) "Idealism and Materialism in Clarín's *La Regenta* : Two Comparative Studies", *Revue de Littérature Comparée*, XLIV (1970), 273-95, is of great interest. The journal *Archivum* (Oviedo) has, over the years, published articles on various aspects of the novel.

None of the small handful of books on Alas as a novelist has much to commend it. The only published attempt at a comprehensive account has been Albert Brent's (*21*) *Leopoldo Alas and "La Regenta"* (University of Missouri, 1951), in which a few worthwhile points are made in a somewhat laboured way. E. J.

Gramberg, *(22)* *Fondo y forma del humorismo de Leopoldo Alas, Clarín* (Oviedo, 1958), Jean Bécarud, *(23)* *"La Regenta" de Clarín y la Restauración* (Madrid, 1964), and Juan Ventura Agudiez, *(24)* *Inspiración y estética en la "Regenta" de Clarín* (Oviedo, 1970), are even more laboured and less worthwhile. Juan Antonio Cabezas, *(25)* *Clarín, el provinciano universal* (Madrid, 1962), is a florid and unreliable biography.